VOYAGES IN ENGLISH

Writing and Grammar

Grade 6 Practice Book

Elaine de Chantal Brookes

Patricia Healey

Irene Kervick

Catherine Irene Masino

Anne B. McGuire

Adrienne Saybolt

LOYOLAPRESS.

ISBN: 0-8294-2095-9

LOYOLAPRESS.
3441 N. ASHLAND AVENUE
CHICAGO, ILLINOIS 60657
(800) 621-1008
www.LoyolaPress.org

05 06 07 08 09 10 11 12 13 14 VH 10 9 8 7 6 5 4 3 2 1

CONTENTS

CHAPTER 5

Writing: Expository Writing
Grammar: Verbs, Adverbs

CHAPTER 6

Writing: Business Letters
Grammar: Parts of Sentences

CHAPTER 7

Writing: Creative Writing (Trickster Tales)
Grammar: Conjunctions, Interjections, Punctuation, and Capitalization

CHAPTER 8

Writing: Research Reports
Grammar: Diagramming

CHAPTER 1

Singular and Plural Nouns

● **Write the plural form of each noun.**

1. dish _____

2. wolf _____

3. country _____

4. fly _____

5. valley _____

6. batch _____

7. thief _____

8. horse _____

9. peach _____

10. glass _____

11. prairie _____

12. chimney _____

13. knife _____

14. box _____

● **Now find each plural noun that you listed above in the word search below. The words can be horizontal, vertical, or diagonal.**

```
A  L  P  G  H  B  O  P  R  A  I  R  I  E  S  W  R  Y
P  L  E  X  I  F  H  D  T  N  B  A  T  C  H  E  S  U
N  O  A  G  L  L  W  C  I  M  C  S  T  H  O  N  N  A
J  O  C  T  H  I  E  V  E  S  I  N  G  I  R  K  S  T
H  U  H  W  T  E  B  K  H  I  H  N  V  M  S  I  B  S
P  A  E  N  O  S  G  L  A  S  S  E  S  N  E  M  O  M
G  H  S  C  H  L  K  N  I  V  E  S  S  E  S  W  X  Y
K  O  T  T  B  N  V  A  L  L  E  Y  S  Y  U  R  E  S
C  O  U  N  T  R  I  E  S  H  R  T  M  S  W  P  S  P
Y  R  N  T  O  C  V  E  S  R  N  I  E  N  R  K  S  A
```

CHAPTER 1

More Singular and Plural Nouns

● **Underline the singular noun in each sentence. Write the plural form on the line.**

1. My brother plays the piano. _____

2. One person sat under the trees. _____

3. That woman has two jobs. _____

4. The tooth appeared to be white with sharp edges. _____

5. An ox strained against the ropes. _____

6. Some tourists saw a moose standing in the reeds. _____

7. The women thought they saw a mouse. _____

8. I am my younger brother's hero. _____

9. My brother-in-law treats many patients. _____

10. A single salmon swam over the rocks. _____

● **Use the plural nouns you wrote above to complete the sentences below. Use context clues to determine where each plural noun belongs.**

11. The jury was made up of seven men and five _____.

12. Because she has two married sisters, Marina now has two _____.

13. Grandma owns two grand _____.

14. Many _____ cheered as the winners were announced.

15. _____ had chewed tiny holes in the corner of the cereal box.

16. Several _____ pulled the heavy wagon.

17. _____ migrate upstream to lay their eggs.

18. Many people have _____ they look up to.

19. A shark's mouth contains rows of sharp _____.

20. Many _____ travel in herds across Canada.

CHAPTER 1

What Makes a Good Personal Narrative?

● **Read the personal narrative. Then answer the questions.**

Have you ever seen an alligator in the wild? The only alligator I had ever seen was in photographs. Then on our trip to Florida, we traveled a road called Alligator Alley through the Everglades. Once we were on it, I thought, I wonder if we'll actually see an alligator from the highway? Well, I discovered that we could! I not only saw one alligator but many alligators. They looked like muddy black slabs of clay drying in the warm sun along the banks of the canal. Egrets were wading in the shallow water. I certainly didn't want to get any closer.

1. Underline the sentence that is the narrative's introduction. Write another introduction for this narrative that might attract the reader's attention.

   _____

2. From what point of view is this paragraph written? How can you tell?

   _____

3. Which of the following best describes the order of the body in this paragraph?

   a. travel through Alligator Alley, wonder about alligators, see many alligators

   b. see many alligators, can't see their faces, travel through Florida

   c. travel through Alligator Alley, alligators drying, see many alligators

4. Which sentence does not relate well to the writer's topic?

   _____

5. Which sentence acts as the conclusion for the narrative?

   _____

   _____

Count and Noncount Nouns

● **Write _N_ if the underlined word is a noncount noun or _C_ if it is a count noun.**

1. A heavy <u>smog</u> settled over the city. _____

2. City <u>workers</u> recently planted new grass in our park. _____

3. The sand on the <u>beach</u> was too hot for their feet. _____

4. The <u>scientist</u> was known for her great intelligence. _____

5. Several dumpsters were overflowing with <u>garbage</u>. _____

6. The new treaty established <u>peace</u> between the countries. _____

7. A puddle was formed by the flowing <u>water</u>. _____

8. My father steamed the rice in a <u>pan</u> on the stove. _____

9. Antique <u>furniture</u> crowded the room. _____

10. This holiday celebrates the <u>independence</u> of our country. _____

11. The oil on the <u>road</u> caused the car to skid. _____

12. After the activity the students cleaned the <u>equipment</u>. _____

● **Not every noncount above is underlined. Find the rest. Then classify every noncount noun in the sentences above into one of the following categories.**

Gas or Liquid	Made of Tiny Parts	Collection of Things	Abstract Noun
_____	_____	_____	_____
_____	_____	_____	_____
_____	_____	_____	_____

Concrete and Abstract Nouns

● **Write *C* if the underlined noun is a concrete noun. Write *A* if it is abstract.**

1. Take care of your <u>health</u> by exercising regularly. _____

2. The <u>map</u> is torn apart. _____

3. We had <u>hope</u> that we would win. _____

4. Overwhelming <u>happiness</u> spread throughout the crowd. _____

5. The tall building is made of <u>steel</u>. _____

6. A young <u>girl</u> raced past us. _____

7. Rosa felt <u>regret</u> for hurting May. _____

8. Help me put the <u>pennies</u> in the sacks. _____

9. Africa is a large <u>continent</u>. _____

10. Thank you for your <u>kindness</u>. _____

11. Tom was filled with <u>awe</u> as he gazed at the tornado in his path. _____

● **Draw an illustration to show the meaning of the abstract nouns below.**

Laughter	Bravery

CHAPTER 1 Introductions and Conclusions

● **Tell what you might expect to learn in a paragraph that uses each of the following as its introductory sentence.**

1. By the end of the day, the mysterious cat I met had caused the most tumultuous event of my life.

_____

_____

2. The black flag with the skull and crossbones and the hulking ghost of a ship both signaled one thing to me—pirates!

_____

_____

3. Among the bright lights, chatter of voices, clinking dishes, and people rushing around, I felt completely lost during my older sister's big event.

_____

_____

● **For each personal narrative subject, write the letter of the matching conclusion.**

4. a narrative about a sporting event _____

5. a personal narrative about a speech _____

6. a narrative report about a club's event _____

a. However, as nervous as I was, I had looked my audience in the eye, spoken clearly, and gestured as I talked. All of my practice had paid off.

b. The team's incredible victory was the perfect ending to my first game as captain.

c. As you can see, the funds raised, the recruiting of new members, and the involvement of our current members all helped make this event a success.

● **Choose a personal narrative subject from above or one of your own. On a separate sheet of paper, plan the narrative by using a Narrative Map like the one on page 137.**

CHAPTER 1

Nouns as Subjects and Subject Complements

- **For each sentence write the subject noun and its complement in the correct columns.**

	Subject	Complement
1. A scroll is a roll of paper.	_____	_____
2. Many books are paperback copies.	_____	_____
3. Shakespeare was a famous playwright.	_____	_____
4. The older daughter is an avid reader.	_____	_____
5. Someday Gary may be an author.	_____	_____
6. Mrs. Lopez is a writing teacher.	_____	_____
7. My uncle is a vegetarian.	_____	_____
8. The final event was the downhill race.	_____	_____

- **For each word write two sentences. In the first sentence use the word as a subject noun. In the second sentence use the same word as a subject complement.**

9. skates

_____

_____

10. painting

_____

_____

CHAPTER 1

Nouns as Objects

● Circle the letter under the heading that correctly identifies the underlined word. Then write the letters on the corresponding lines below. If your answers are correct, you will spell a sentence.

	Direct Object	Indirect Object	Object of a Preposition
1. The storm clouds brought our <u>city</u> heavy rains.	M	N	O
2. The students sold my grandfather raffle <u>tickets</u>.	A	I	R
3. Mr. Jenson read a mystery story to the <u>class</u>.	T	P	M
4. Dina handed the new <u>student</u> a pencil.	C	E	Q
5. We sent our cousins a <u>letter</u>.	A	H	B
6. The magician taught the audience a <u>trick</u>.	L	O	E
7. I bought a present for my <u>brother</u>.	W	T	L
8. Kelly owed her <u>sister</u> a favor.	K	N	C
9. My parents sold Gail the <u>automobile</u>.	O	E	G
10. The waiter brought the <u>woman</u> a bowl of soup.	T	U	D
11. The whole class wrote the principal a get-well <u>letter</u>.	N	H	F
12. Jamie sang a song about his <u>grandmother</u>.	T	X	S

● After you write the circled letters on the lines below, work with a partner to do what the sentence says.

___ ___ ___ ___ ___ ___ ___ ___ ___ ___ ___ ___.
1   2   3   4   5   6   7   8   9   10 11 12

CHAPTER 1 Dictionary

● **Use the guide words on the dictionary pages to identify on which page you would find each word. Write the page number on the line. If your answers are correct, you will reveal the answer to the riddle below.**

1. flexible   page _____

2. fluster   page _____

3. flagrant   page _____

4. fitness   page _____

5. fraught   page _____

6. flabbergast page _____

7. filibuster   page _____

8. flute   page _____

9. fiasco   page _____

10. feign   page _____

11. foundation page _____

● **Now find the capital letter on the dictionary page that corresponds with each page number. Write each letter on the matching line.**

Who likes to be called Miss but never Ms. or Mrs.?

Answer: ___ ___ ___ ___ ___ ___ ___ ___ ___ ___ ___
           1   2   3   4   5   6   7   8   9 10 11

● **Place the words from the list above in alphabetical order.**

1. _____   5. _____   9. _____

2. _____   6. _____   10. _____

3. _____   7. _____   11. _____

4. _____   8. _____

Possessive Nouns

● **Write the singular possessive form and the plural possessive form of each noun.**

1. baby   _____   _____

2. child   _____   _____

3. horse   _____   _____

4. wolf   _____   _____

5. mouse   _____   _____

● **Use each phrase to write a possessive noun. Then draw a sketch to show what each possessive phrase means.**

6. friend of Amy _____friend	7. song of the sparrows _____song
8. paintings of the artists _____ paintings	9. recipe of the chef _____ recipe

CHAPTER 1

Nouns Showing Separate and Joint Possession

● **Rewrite each expression to show separate or joint possession. The first one is done for you.**

1. the books shared by Molly and Nick

   _Molly and Nick's books_____

2. Mrs. Sims and Mrs. Cortez each have a baby.

   _____

3. the tail of the horse and the tail of the dog

   _____

4. the vacation that Taylor and Keesha took together

   _____

5. the car that my mother and father own

   _____

6. the house of Eva is near the house of Paulo

   _____

● **Use the information in each sentence to write a phrase that shows separate or joint possession. Draw a sketch for each sentence to illustrate how it shows possession.**

7. Stan and Kari share a bicycle. _____	8. Alan owns a bicycle and so does Phong. _____

CHAPTER 1

Revising Sentences

● **Improve these rambling or run-on sentences. You may add or change words to make your improved sentences read smoothly. Then draw a sketch that illustrates your rewritten sentences.**

1. The young boy threw the ball hard, and his dog Scruffy energetically began the chase over a rock and under a picnic table, and just when he was about to grab the ball it bounced against a tree and sailed past the startled dog's head.

_____

_____

_____

_____

_____

_____

_____

_____

2. There were too many cooks in the kitchen my sister Martha was stirring the pancake mix while Dennis tried not to pour too much juice into the glasses Dad maneuvered the dishes to the table as the dog and cat wandered about waiting for some food to come their way.

_____

_____

_____

_____

_____

_____

_____

_____

_____

CHAPTER 1
Appositives

● Use the noun phrases in the box to add appositives to the following sentences. Use context clues to match each appositive to the correct sentence. Then underline the noun that each appositive explains.

> a furry, brown hamster   the Sunshine State   my lucky charm
>
> her favorite dessert   an explorer   the soccer coach
>
> our English teacher   a bicycle race   a cold soup
>
> a doctor

1. We vacationed in Florida, _____.

2. The Tour de France, _____, has cyclists from all over the world.

3. Meriwether Lewis, _____, recorded information about the Louisiana Purchase.

4. I held onto the locket, _____.

5. Mr. Davis, _____, set up the goal on Saturday morning.

6. Susan Robinson, _____, sees many patients every day.

7. We had a cup of gazpacho, _____, for lunch.

8. Paul shared his pet, _____, with the class.

9. We read *The Cay* at the request of Mrs. Levenson, _____.

10. I baked my mom a cake, _____.

CHAPTER 1

Words Used as Nouns and Verbs

● **Use each word in the box to complete two of the sentences below. For each sentence, write *noun* or *verb* to show how the word is used.**

| skate | paint | shade | step | book | head |

1. It's muddy, so watch where you _____! _____

2. The blade on his _____ needed sharpening. _____

3. Mariah can _____ without effort across the ice. _____

4. The top _____ of the staircase is icy. _____

5. Lila sat in the _____ under the tree. _____

6. The visor will _____ your eyes from the light. _____

7. I usually _____ with watercolors. _____

8. She just finished reading a good _____. _____

9. The Lincolns may _____ a flight to Chicago. _____

10. Thomas shook his _____ up and down. _____

11. Clark chose green _____ for the walls. _____

12. After this left turn, we will _____ for the beach. _____

● **Choose one word from the box above and use it in two sentences, once as a noun and once as a verb.**

_____

_____

CHAPTER

1

Exact Words

● **For each underlined word, write a more exact word to replace it.
Then write a sentence that illustrates your more precise word
choice. The first one is done for you.**

1. The parent was <u>happy</u>.   The parent was ____ecstatic____.

   <u>The parent was ecstatic when both of her children earned straight A's.</u>

2. It was a <u>good</u> movie   It was a _____ movie.

   _____

   _____

3. He <u>walks</u> through the alley.   He _____ through the alley.

   _____

   _____

4. I <u>made</u> a mask.   I _____ a mask.

   _____

   _____

5. My cousin said the party was <u>nice</u>.   My cousin said the party was _____.

   _____

   _____

6. The <u>picture</u> was <u>funny</u>.   The _____ was _____.

   _____

   _____

CHAPTER
1

Words Used as Nouns and Adjectives

● Select the appropriate word from the box to use as a noun and as an adjective in each pair of sentences. Write *ADJ* when the word is used as an adjective and *N* when it is used as a noun.

> birthday   car   plant   cotton   chocolate

1. The Flores family attended the antique _____ show at the convention center.   _____

   The _____ was packed and ready for the trip.   _____

2. Mom bought this begonia at the _____ sale on Sunday.   _____

   The banana _____ grew five feet that season.   _____

3. Tina's _____ is a week from Tuesday.   _____

   She will invite ten guests to her _____ party.   _____

4. Jose's favorite beverage is _____ milk.   _____

   _____ comes from the pod of a plant.   _____

5. The boy's jacket was made from a blend of wool and _____.   _____

   The quilt was sewn from a printed _____ fabric.   _____

● For each word write one sentence that uses it as a noun and another sentence that uses it as an adjective.

6. plastic

   _____

   _____

7. horse

   _____

   _____

Name_____ Date_____

Self-Assessment

● Check *Always*, *Sometimes*, or *Never* to respond to each statement.

Writing	Always	Sometimes	Never
I can identify a personal narrative and its features.			
I understand how to write an effective introduction and conclusion for a personal narrative.			
I can use a dictionary.			
I can revise run-on and rambling sentences so that they are correct.			
I use exact words so that my writing is clear and effective.			

Grammar	Always	Sometimes	Never
I can identify and use singular and plural nouns.			
I can identify and use irregular nouns.			
I can identify and use count and noncount nouns.			
I can identify and use concrete and abstract nouns.			
I can identify and use nouns as subjects and subject complements.			
I can identify and use nouns as objects.			
I can identify and use possessive nouns.			
I can show joint possession with nouns.			
I can identify and use appositives.			
I can identify words used as nouns and as verbs and use them correctly.			
I can identify words used as nouns and as adjectives and use them correctly.			

● **Write the most helpful thing you learned in this chapter.**

_____

_____

CHAPTER

2 Personal Pronouns

● **Circle the pronoun in each sentence. Then write all the words from the box that describe that pronoun. Remember that only third person singular pronouns have gender.**

first person	second person	third person
singular	plural	
masculine	feminine	neuter

1. They biked for two hours before tiring.

    a. _____   b. _____

2. Sarina told us about the soccer game.

    a. _____   b. _____

3. We saw a large opossum in the park.

    a. _____   b. _____

4. She declared that today was the best day of summer vacation.

    a. _____   b. _____   c. _____

5. You were the first person to get the right answer.

    a. _____   b. _____

6. Evidently, the judge did not believe him.

    a. _____   b. _____   c. _____

7. I asked Dad about the problem.

    a. _____   b. _____

8. It hit the ground with force.

    a. _____   b. _____   c. _____

9. Were the instructions meant for them?

    a. _____   b. _____

10. Tell her not to worry about the campout.

    a. _____   b. _____   c. _____

CHAPTER 2

Agreement of Pronouns and Antecedents

● **Choose the pronoun from the word box that best completes each sentence. Then draw an arrow from the pronoun to its antecedent.**

it	they	them	you	I	we
us	she	her	he	him	me

1. My father walks in the park at sunset. _____ is a quiet, peaceful place.

2. Our class didn't like the questions on the test. _____ were very difficult to answer.

3. Jerry and I read the note. Was the message meant for _____ ?

4. The pasta in the bowl looked delicious. The smell of _____ made us hungry.

5. Anna needs paint and brushes. Give the supplies to _____ .

6. My grandfather collects stamps and coins. _____ has many valuable ones.

7. Teresa had an appointment with the dentist. _____ had no cavities.

8. The judges announced the winners at the fair. Ribbons were given to _____ .

9. My dad plays in a band. _____ plays the saxophone very well.

10. The magician invited Sam and me onto the stage. _____ helped perform several tricks.

CHAPTER 2

What Makes a Good How-to Article?

● **Write an *X* next to each idea that is important to remember when writing a good how-to article.**

1. Give directions that are appropriate for your audience. _____

2. Be sure steps are presented in order. _____

3. Always begin your introduction with a difficult question. _____

4. Be sure directions are clear and concise. _____

5. Don't use imperative sentences. _____

6. Use accurate details so the reader knows exactly what to do. _____

7. Warn the reader of any problems he or she may encounter. _____

8. Describe the characters, using colorful adjectives. _____

9. Before you write, review the steps yourself so you know what to include. _____

10. Use dialog to help the reader understand the plot. _____

● **Imagine that you are writing about how to wrap a boxed gift. Rewrite each direction to provide a more accurate and complete step. You can use more than one sentence as you revise. The first one is done for you.**

11. Cut the wrapping paper.

   Cut the wrapping paper several inches longer and wider than the box.

12. Wrap the box.

   _____

13. Seal the paper with tape.

   _____

14. Add a bow.

   _____

15. Attach a card.

   _____

CHAPTER 2

Intensive and Reflexive Pronouns

● **Circle the reflexive or intensive pronoun in each sentence. Write** *reflexive* **or** *intensive* **to identify the type of pronoun. Underline the antecedent in each sentence.**

1. The statue itself was found about 300 years ago.　　　_____

2. Macy found the way to the entrance herself.　　　_____

3. The explorer himself described the strange markings.　　　_____

4. The students and I explored the new cave ourselves.　　　_____

5. Thomas and Maria, please finish the puzzle yourselves.　　　_____

6. The markings themselves looked like a foreign language.　　　_____

7. Many people wanted the jewels for themselves.　　　_____

8. The scientists found themselves a copy of the map.　　　_____

9. Mario cut himself a piece of cake.　　　_____

10. You yourself know how to do it.　　　_____

CHAPTER 2 Subject Pronouns

● **Read each sentence. Replace each underlined antecedent with the correct pronoun from the chart and rewrite the sentence. Then write the corresponding number for the pronoun in the box. The first one is done for you.**

us	we	you	he	she	it	they	her
28	33	17	11	31	15	9	30

1. <u>My family and I</u> went on vacation.

   We went on vacation._____   ☐ 33

2. The winner of the contest was <u>Renee</u>.

   _____   ☐

3. <u>You and Terry</u> had better get started on your project.

   _____   ☐

4. <u>The boys on the swim team</u> traveled to Montreal, Canada.

   _____   ☐

5. <u>The museum director</u> closed the door to his office.

   _____   ☐

6. My fifth-grade teacher was <u>Mrs. Jackson</u>.

   _____   ☐

7. <u>The ornate brass box</u> has been in my family for generations.

   _____   ☐

8. Where in the world were <u>Jamie and I</u>?

   _____   ☐

9. <u>The curious children</u> played with the new equipment.

   _____   ☐

10. The next people in line are <u>Dad and you</u>.

   _____   ☐

● **Now add up the numbers in the boxes. If your answers are correct, your sum should match the number of bones in an adult human body.**

Number of bones = _____

CHAPTER 2 Order, Accuracy, and Completeness

● **Number the sentences from 1 to 6 to place the directions in the correct order.**

1.

Cake Mix Directions
_____ Cool the cake completely before frosting it.
_____ Bake for 30 minutes at 350 degrees Farenheit.
_____ Pour the batter into a 9" x 11" greased cake pan.
_____ Stir 1 cup water, 2 eggs, and 1/2 cup oil into the dry mix to form a batter.
_____ Beat the batter on low speed for about 2 minutes.
_____ Pour the dry cake mix into a large bowl.

● **Read each pair of sentences. Circle the letter of the sentence that is more accurate or complete.**

2. a. Separate some eggs and add to the milk mixture.

   b. Separate four eggs and add the yolks to the milk mixture.

3. a. Turn the bolt counterclockwise for six turns, using a small crescent wrench.

   b. Adjust the bolt a few turns with a small wrench.

4. a. Use a medium putty knife to apply spackling compound to any holes.

   b. With a flat tool, repair all cracks or holes.

5. a. Don't forget to water the plants three times a day.

   b. Water the seedlings in the morning, at noon, and in the evening.

6. a. Fill a pan with water and set the mirror in the pan at an angle.

   b. Place the mirror at a 45-degree angle in 1 inch of water in a shallow pan.

CHAPTER

2 Object Pronouns

- **Underline the object pronoun in each sentence. If the pronoun is used as a direct object, write *DO*. If it is used as an indirect object, write *IO*. Write *OP* if the pronoun is an object of a preposition.**

1. The clerk handed the receipt to us. _____
2. The drama teacher offered me the best part. _____
3. Bill passed her the completed paper. _____
4. The runner quickly raced in front of them. _____
5. Did Jake take Ari and him to the office? _____
6. Our teacher handed him the largest book. _____
7. Mrs. Grazie asked you to be quiet. _____
8. The woman gave Irina and me a book of poetry. _____
9. The usher pointed out the exit to them. _____
10. Kerri wants to teach sign language to you. _____
11. Shari will send me the letter. _____
12. Why didn't you tell us about the prize? _____
13. Joe has a new dog, but I have not seen it. _____
14. Ryan played the piano for us. _____

A
B
C
D
E
F
G

- **Look through a novel. Find three different sentences that use an object pronoun. Write each sentence. Ask a partner to find the object pronoun in each.**

_____

_____

_____

_____

CHAPTER 2

Possessive Pronouns and Adjectives

- **Underline the possessive pronoun in each set of sentences. Circle the possessive adjective in each set.**

1. This is my pencil. Yours fell on the floor.

2. The barking dog is hers. Your dog is so well behaved!

3. He doesn't have his papers. Give him one of theirs.

4. Our boat is here. We saw theirs at the marina.

5. The squirrel flicked its tail. The birdseed it was eating wasn't ours.

- **Read the paragraph. Cross out the six possessive pronouns or adjectives that are used incorrectly. Write the correct form of each word in the margin at the end of the line.**

"I believe that is mine," said Courtney, spying the coin I held in mine hand.

"Why would the coin be your?" I asked. "You've been in class all morning."

She blinked, unsure of what to say. Several students walked by, deep in conversation.

"After all," I rationalized, "it might even be their."

"Look, it's my coin," Courtney whined. "Are you going to give it to me or not?"

I glanced down at my palm and concealed my surprise. There was no image on it surface. The coin was only a disk of metal. "Tell you what, Courtney, you're right. It must be yours coin." I tossed it in hers direction. I walked away before she realized what had become hers.

CHAPTER 2

Transition Words

● **Underline seven transition words and phrases in the directions. (Hint: The first transition word is *Begin*.)**

Begin making your rubber-band banjo by cutting a hole in a shoebox lid. Next, tape the lid securely to the box. After that, cut two wood strips the same width as your box and glue one strip to each end of the box. While the glue is drying, arrange the rubber bands from thinnest to thickest. The next step is to stretch the rubber bands around the box, fitting each band over the strips of wood and across the hole. To finish, make sure none of the bands touch. Now your rubber-band banjo is ready to play!

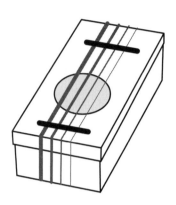

● **Rewrite these directions in paragraph form. Add transition words and phrases to make the directions clear.**

Turn Cream into Play Plastic

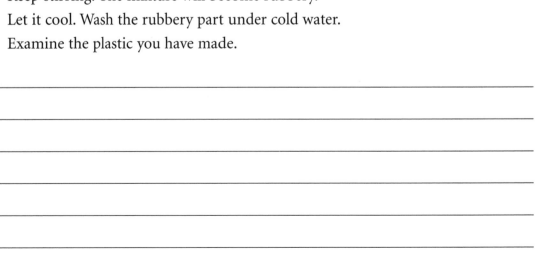

Ask an adult to help you.

Warm a cup of heavy cream in a pot.

Watch for the cream to just start bubbling.

Slowly stir in three to five teaspoons of vinegar.

Keep stirring. The mixture will become rubbery.

Let it cool. Wash the rubbery part under cold water.

Examine the plastic you have made.

_____

_____

_____

_____

_____

CHAPTER 2

Pronouns in Contractions

- **Circle the letter below the word that correctly completes each sentence. If your answers are correct, the circled letters will answer the riddle below.**

1. _____ too late to go to the store.	It's A	Its G
2. _____ very glad that you attended.	We've R	We're N
3. I thought _____ be a lot smaller.	they'll E	they'd T
4. Tyrell said that _____ left already.	they've I	they're E
5. I notice that _____ already noon.	it'll N	it's B
6. I think _____ be pleased with the results.	you've H	you'll I
7. _____ happy to see it is snowing.	I'm O	I'll E
8. _____ be moving to Utah at the end of the month.	He's A	He'll T
9. I think _____ going to win.	she'll R	she's I
10. I think _____ staying in the new hotel.	he's C	he'll T

What medicine do you give a sick insect?

Answer: An ___ ___ ___ - ___ ___ ___ ___ ___ ___ ___
         1   2   3   4   5   6   7   8   9   10

CHAPTER

2

Demonstrative Pronouns

● Complete each sentence with *this, that, these,* or *those.* Use the clue in parentheses to help you choose the correct word. Then circle the noun to which each pronoun refers.

1. _____ is the best sandwich I've ever eaten. (near)

2. _____ are my pictures. (far)

3. _____ is the book I told you about. (near)

4. Is _____ the letter the writer described? (far)

5. _____ are the most unusual rocks. (far)

6. _____ are the chairs she needs in the other room. (near)

7. Weren't _____ the blue balloons Mom wanted for table decorations? (near)

8. After seeing the vase, I decided _____ would make a nice centerpiece. (far)

9. _____ is the ring my grandfather gave me. (near)

10. _____ looks like the coat I bought last month. (far)

● Now find the nouns you circled above in the word search below. The words can be horizontal, vertical, or diagonal.

```
O  H  E  S  D  A  A  Y  P  I  C  T  U  R  E  S  C  L  A
B  N  T  Y  O  T  U  M  S  C  L  E  A  E  K  B  S  E  Y
V  O  S  A  N  D  W  I  C  H  T  O  H  C  E  G  L  T  D
A  A  O  W  B  N  A  S  L  A  E  L  O  A  O  R  O  T  L
S  Y  N  K  L  S  I  W  G  I  H  R  I  N  G  T  P  E  W
E  H  A  O  T  N  S  G  O  R  C  P  R  K  O  S  U  R  D
L  W  B  A  L  L  O  O  N  S  E  C  O  A  T  H  A  V  L
```

CHAPTER 2 Sentence Types

● **Identify the type of each sentence by writing** *simple, compound,* **or** *complex.*

1. My sister belongs to the neighborhood book club. _____

2. The sun was hot, but the breeze kept us cool. _____

3. After scoring the goal, our team won the game. _____

4. I studied hard, yet I couldn't remember how to spell the word. _____

5. Since Ann missed the bus, she was late to class. _____

6. Before I can spend my money, I need to pay back my brother. _____

● **For each box, write a different kind of sentence about a close friend.**

7. Simple: _____
_____
_____
_____

8. Compound: _____
_____
_____
_____

9. Complex: _____
_____
_____
_____

CHAPTER 2

Interrogative Pronouns

● Write *who, whom, whose, what,* or *which* to correctly complete each question. Then answer the questions in complete sentences.

1. In your class _____ last name begins with the letter *S*?

   _____

2. _____ of these men served as our 40th president?

   _____

3. _____ is the capital of North Dakota?

   _____

4. _____ wrote the Declaration of Independence?

   _____

5. _____ did you talk to on the phone last night?

   _____

6. _____ of the cookies do you prefer?

   _____

7. To _____ did you last send a letter?

   _____

8. _____ invented the light bulb?

   _____

CHAPTER 2

Indefinite Pronouns

● **Underline the indefinite pronoun in each sentence. Write whether each pronoun is *singular* or *plural*.**

1. Each won a prize in the contest.   _____

2. Several were disqualified early.   _____

3. I could not get anything done because of the noise.   _____

4. I think everyone wants to play.   _____

5. A few did not want to attend the meeting.   _____

6. Nobody witnessed the accident.   _____

7. Either is talented enough to win the contest.   _____

8. Both shared a locker with me.   _____

9. All of my shoes are old and worn.   _____

10. The professor suspects something.   _____

11. Anyone could answer that question.   _____

● **Now write the first letter of each indefinite pronoun you underlined above the corresponding numbers. If your answers are correct, you will reveal the answer to the trivia question.**

What is the 37th state and the home of the Cornhuskers?

Answer: T h ___ ___ t ___ t ___ o ___ ___ ___ ___ r ___ ___ k ___
           1   2   3   4   5   6 7 8   9 10 11

Instructional Graphics

● **Read the following directions for operating a clothes dryer. Then fill in the flowchart, using the information from the directions.**

1. Place clothes in dryer.

2. Set number of minutes. Push "On."

3. Remove clothes promptly when buzzer sounds.

4. If dryer does not run, check that door is closed and plug is in socket.

5. If dryer still does not run, call service technician.

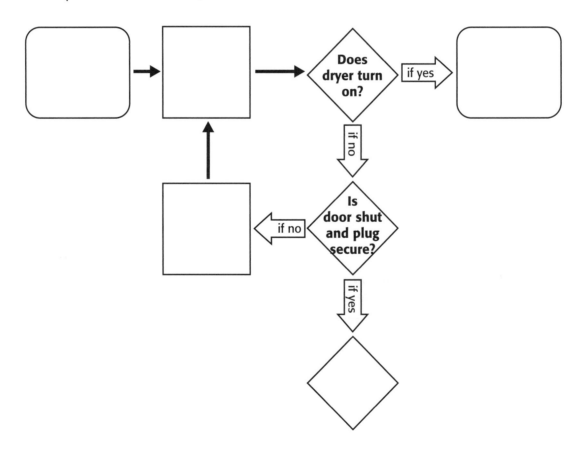

● **Study the Problem/Solution Chart on page 140. Copy a blank version of this instructional graphic on a separate sheet of paper. Fill in the graphic to show how you once tried to solve a problem.**

CHAPTER 2

Indefinite Pronouns and Double Negatives

● **Rewrite each incorrect sentence to correct the use of negatives and indefinite pronouns. If a sentence is correct, write *correct* on the line.**

1. I didn't see nobody at the front door.

   _____

2. The fruit basket didn't have anything in it.

   _____

3. Nobody did not want to go to rehearsal that day.

   _____

4. There was not nothing that could have been done.

   _____

5. Wouldn't no one like to read his or her story to the class?

   _____

6. The children couldn't decide on nothing to play.

   _____

7. I could not see over anybody in front of me.

   _____

8. No one will help you if you don't ask.

   _____

9. Can't nobody figure out the next step in these directions?

   _____

10. I did not like nothing about the book I just read.

   _____

Self-Assessment

● Check *Always*, *Sometimes*, or *Never* to respond to each statement.

Writing	Always	Sometimes	Never
I can identify a how-to article and its features.			
I understand how to use correct order and include accurate and complete information in a how-to article.			
I use transition words so directions are easy to follow.			
I vary the types of sentences I use.			
I can use an instructional graphic to present information and directions.			
I include all the key features when I write a how-to article.			

Grammar	Always	Sometimes	Never
I can identify and use the correct pronoun to show person, number, and gender.			
I can show agreement between pronouns and their antecedents.			
I can identify and use intensive and reflexive pronouns.			
I can identify and use subject pronouns.			
I can identify and use object pronouns.			
I can identify and use possessive pronouns and adjectives.			
I can identify and use pronouns in contractions.			
I can identify and use demonstrative pronouns.			
I can identify and use interrogative pronouns.			
I can identify and use indefinite pronouns.			
I can identify indefinite pronouns and avoid double negatives.			

● **Write the most useful thing you learned in this chapter.**

_____

_____

CHAPTER 3

Descriptive Adjectives

● **Find the adjective in each sentence and write it on the line. Then underline the noun that each adjective modifies.**

1. Maryjane knows a skillful potter. _____

2. Do you enjoy sweet bread? _____

3. The green monster will chase Steve. _____

4. Drowsy Teri slept in class. _____

5. The rich miner found gold and gems. _____

6. Huge oxen broke through the gate. _____

7. Kira flashed a wide grin. _____

8. The vase is made of Swedish crystal. _____

9. The flimsy carton fell apart. _____

10. Robby likes Greek food. _____

● **Now search a newspaper for three descriptive adjectives. List them and the nouns they modify on the lines below.**

11. _____ (adjective) _____ (noun)

12. _____ (adjective) _____ (noun)

13. _____ (adjective) _____ (noun)

CHAPTER 3

Definite and Indefinite Articles

● **Underline the article in each sentence. Then write *D* for definite articles or *I* for indefinite articles.**

1. Many kinds of fruit are on the table. _____

2. The Danube is located in Germany. _____

3. Sam is a great soccer player. _____

4. The co-captain is wearing number 51. _____

5. An orange pencil fell out of his backpack. _____

6. We noticed that a train was leaving for Madrid. _____

7. My friends prepared for the party. _____

8. You might want to take an umbrella today. _____

9. The captain asked for our assistance. _____

10. The French bakery has moved. _____

● **Complete each sentence with a definite or an indefinite article.**

11. (definite) _____ player kicked a goal.

12. (indefinite) _____ ugly bug raced across the floor.

13. (indefinite) I felt _____ strong wind at my back.

14. (definite) Did you go to _____ movies last night?

15. (indefinite) James wanted _____ apple for a snack.

16. (definite) She's going to take _____ test now.

17. (indefinite) Yoko went into _____ comic-book shop.

18. (indefinite) _____ insect jumped on Mary.

19. (definite) Kylie swam in _____ lake.

20. (indefinite) I have two cookies and _____ sandwich.

CHAPTER 3

What Makes a Good Description?

● **Read the descriptive paragraph. Then answer the questions.**

> At dawn, the lake looked like a giant sheet of glittering glass. In the distance, fog rose evenly from the surface, signaling a cool morning. Tiny waves lapped against the rocks on shore, echoing a calm, rhythmic beat. There was no breeze, so the pines hovering directly above me were silent. It was at dawn when the lake seemed most lonely, expectant for the coming hours when it would spring to life.

1. For what kind of audience is the writer writing—small children or adults? Why do you think so?

   <u>Adults; because the details are described with words too hard</u>

   <u>for small children</u>

2. Which way did the writer describe the lake, from left to right, from top to bottom, or from far to near? Why do you think so?

   _____

   _____

3. What did the writer do to help you "see" the lake?

   _____

   _____

4. Which sentence included a sensory detail that helped you "hear" the lake?

   _____

   _____

5. Which vivid adjectives and verbs are most appealing to you? Why?

   _____

● **One way to plan a description can be to compare and contrast two topics. Copy a blank version of the Compare and Contrast Chart on page 138. Choose two related topics. Fill in the chart with descriptive words and phrases.**

CHAPTER 3
Numerical Adjectives

● **Circle the numerical adjective that correctly completes each sentence. Then write the noun that the circled adjective modifies.**

1. The (one first) day of April is Saturday. _____

2. We have attended (six sixth) games so far. _____

3. Matt hit a home run on the (three third) pitch. _____

4. He rounded all (four fourth) bases at a quick pace. _____

5. I asked for (two second) scoops of ice cream in my sundae. _____

6. Our neighbors are going camping in (twelve twelfth) days. _____

7. The black horse took (four fourth) place in the race. _____

8. There are (five fifth) people riding in that car. _____

● **Choose five numerical adjectives from above and use each one in a sentence of your own.**

9. _____

_____

10. _____

_____

11. _____

_____

12. _____

_____

13. _____

_____

CHAPTER 3

Adjectives as Subject Complements

● Circle the letter under *Before* if the underlined adjective comes before the noun it modifies. Circle the letter under *Complement* if the adjective is a subject complement. Use your answers to solve the sentence below.

	Before	Complement
1. The Taj Mahal in India is an <u>exquisite</u> building.	G	W
2. These streets are <u>narrow</u>.	E	R
3. Leo's teacher is <u>kind</u> and helpful.	L	A
4. Nancy heard a <u>weird</u> noise.	M	I
5. We gazed upon the <u>dusty</u> desert.	M	L
6. The storm was <u>violent</u> and swift.	N	A
7. Can you name the <u>smallest</u> ocean?	R	P
8. Paul traveled through the <u>Italian</u> vineyards.	I	B
9. The roses are <u>fragrant</u>.	G	S
10. Becky is planning a <u>big</u> party.	F	R
11. <u>Twenty</u> guards surrounded the prisoner.	U	Y
12. The Assyrian rulers were <u>firm</u>.	O	N

Sentence: ___ ___ ___ ___ ___ ___ ___   ___ ___   ___ ___ ___.
         1 2 3 4 5 6 7   8 9   10 11 12

● **Now go back and circle the noun each adjective modifies.**

CHAPTER

3 Writing a Description

● **Read the description from *Knots in My Yo-yo String* by Jerry Spinelli. Then circle the letter for the best answer to each question.**

> Each year at the end of summer vacation, I rubbed my glove with olive oil from the kitchen cabinet. Then I pressed a baseball deep into the pocket of the glove, curled the leather fingers about the ball, and squeezed the whole thing into a shoebox. Standing on a chair, I set the box high on a closet shelf. Baseball season was officially over.

1. On what sense does the author focus in his description?

   a. touch

   b. smell

2. In what way is the description organized?

   a. from left to right

   b. from first step to last step in a process

● **Write the details that show the paragraph's organization on a Sequencing graphic organizer. The first step is done for you. For an example of a sequencing chart, see page 139.**

End of Baseball Season

> 1. rubbed glove with olive oil

> 2.

> 3.

> 4.

> 5.

CHAPTER 3

Comparative and Superlative Adjectives

● **Write the correct comparative or superlative form of the adjective to complete the sentence. Then draw a sketch to show what each sentence means.**

1. young Nathan is the _____ child of the four children in his family.	2. shady The maple tree is _____ than the pine tree.
3. valuable (more or most) That diamond ring is the _____ ring in the case.	4. good The red pants look _____ than the gray ones.
5. big Tom has the _____ shoes in class.	6. comfortable (less or least) The chair is _____ than the couch.

More Comparative and Superlative Adjectives

● **Circle the letter of the adjective that correctly completes each sentence. Then write the circled letters on the lines below to answer the riddle.**

1. Jenna is _____ than Mary.
   s. tall
   l. taller
   v. tallest

2. We live in the _____ town in the county.
   t. safe
   p. safer
   a. safest

3. Yolanda is quite _____ .
   n. slim
   g. slimmer
   w. slimmest

4. The hammer is _____ than the saw.
   c. noisy
   d. noisier
   m. noisiest

5. He is the _____ actor I have ever met.
   a. famous
   j. more famous
   r. most famous

6. I can run _____ than you can.
   k. far
   m. farther
   t. farthest

7. Her hair is quite _____ .
   t. pretty
   b. prettier
   l. prettiest

8. That is the _____ tiger I have ever seen!
   u. tame
   r. tamer
   t. tamest

Where do dogs do their wash?

Answer: The __ __ u __ __ __ o __ u __ __
           1 2   3 4 5   6   7 8

CHAPTER

Sensory Language

● **Read each sentence. Write *S* if the comparison is a simile. Write *M* if the comparison is a metaphor. Write *N* if there is no comparison.**

1. The cat's tongue was like sandpaper.   _____

2. The biting wind was a slap in the face.   _____

3. Her frightened eyes were as big as saucers.   _____

4. The huge black engine sped down the tracks.   _____

5. The parking lot was an ice rink.   _____

6. Scalding water spilled from the teapot.   _____

7. That snowboarder is like a champion surfer.   _____

8. The nest of chicks was like a bowl of life.   _____

9. A faint glimmer shone through the curtains.   _____

10. The grass was a thick carpet of green.   _____

● **Now choose your favorite simile or metaphor from above. Draw a picture to show what you think it means.**

CHAPTER 3

Little, Less, Least and Few, Fewer, Fewest

● **Write _little_, _less_, _least_, _few_, _fewer_, or _fewest_ to complete each sentence. Then circle the first letter in each word that the adjective modifies. Write the letters on the lines below to create the sentence.**

1. There are _____ yaks than llamas.

2. Jake chose only a _____ oranges to purchase.

3. _____ umbrellas will fit in the other stand.

4. This plant requires the _____ amount of attention.

5. The recipe needs _____ raisins than we first thought.

6. This lamp is the best choice since it uses the _____ energy.

7. Kira's house has _____ windows than Haley's house.

8. I ate _____ ice cream than I thought I would.

9. The _____ students ever qualified for the spelling bee this year.

10. Only a _____ effort is needed to finish painting the room.

Sentence: ___ ___ ___ ___ ___ ___ ___ ___ ___ ___.
             1   2   3   4   5   6   7   8   9 10

CHAPTER 3

Demonstrative Adjectives

● **Underline the demonstrative adjective in each sentence. Write *S* if the demonstrative adjective is singular or *P* if it is plural.**

1. This house is the most beautiful one on the block. _____

2. These sandwiches taste delicious. _____

3. I want to play that game. _____

4. Cara wants to play those kinds of sports. _____

5. This type of car gets great gas mileage. _____

6. What is wrong with that dog? _____

7. These colors are our school colors. _____

8. That tongue twister is tough to say. _____

9. What were those strange sounds? _____

10. John says this backpack belongs to him. _____

● **Now go back and circle all the adjectives that signify that the modified noun is something close to the speaker.**

CHAPTER 3
Misused and Confusing Words

● **Circle the word in parentheses that correctly completes each sentence.**

1. I'm sorry, but I can't (accept except) your gift.

2. (Can May) I go with you?

3. George doesn't feel (good well).

4. Look, (it's its) teeth are huge!

5. (They're Their) friends of my family.

6. Lisa will (set sit) in the recliner.

● **Now use all of the words you *didn't* circle in an original story. Write on a separate sheet of paper if you need more room.**

_____

_____

_____

_____

_____

_____

_____

_____

_____

_____

_____

_____

_____

_____

_____

_____

_____

CHAPTER 3 Interrogative Adjectives

● **Write a noun on each line to complete the sentence. Then underline the interrogative adjective that modifies each noun you wrote.**

1. What _____ grows to be the tallest?

2. Whose _____ is named Sparky?

3. Which _____ needs more time to bake?

4. From which _____ did they arrive?

5. Whose _____ has green spots?

6. What _____ is tastiest?

7. Which _____ do you most like to watch?

8. Whose _____ was an astronaut?

9. In which _____ were you born?

10. Whose _____ is coming home from the hospital?

Write two sentences that use different interrogative adjectives.

11. _____

_____

_____

12. _____

_____

_____

CHAPTER 3

Indefinite Adjectives

● **Complete each sentence with an indefinite adjective from the box. Use each adjective only once. Then circle the noun each adjective modifies.**

any	all	another	both	few
many	much	neither	several	some

1. These plants require _____ care.

2. _____ tired babies needed a nap.

3. There are _____ types of pine trees.

4. I don't have _____ extra money for a snack.

5. _____ children can do handstands.

6. _____ sailors must wear uniforms.

7. I'd like to come back _____ day.

8. Thea wanted _____ role in the play.

9. People can go _____ days without food.

10. _____ parrots never learn to talk.

● **Now compare your answers with a partner's answers to see how the use of different adjectives can change the meaning of a sentence. Discuss the meaning of each sentence.**

CHAPTER 3

Thesaurus

● **Use a thesaurus to find synonyms for the italicized words. Use the synonyms to complete the following sentences. Do not use a synonym more than once. The parts of speech in parentheses are clues for which kinds of words to use.**

meet
1. (verb) I would not like to _____ a bear.

2. (noun) Are you going to the wrestling _____ ?

pelt
3. (noun) The hunter came home with a deer _____ .

4. (verb) I will not _____ snowballs.

harbor
5. (noun) The sailboat sailed into the _____ .

6. (verb) I will _____ the secret forever.

show
7. (verb) Can you _____ me how to fix this?

8. (noun) We have tickets to next week's _____ .

run
9. (verb) I can't _____ any faster.

10. (noun) The ski _____ was icy.

trim
11. (verb) My mom _____ my hair.

12. (noun) The _____ on the painting was blue.

part
13. (noun) We all had a _____ of the pie.

14. (verb) I like to _____ my vegetables from my mashed potatoes.

CHAPTER 3
Adjective Phrases

● **Revise each sentence so the underlined adjective is part of an adjective phrase. The first one is done for you.**

1. <u>Courageous</u> people sailed abroad.

   People with courage sailed abroad.

2. The <u>spring</u> blossoms are a welcome sight.

   _____

3. We'd like to adopt an <u>intelligent</u> dog.

   _____

4. The <u>castle</u> walls were slick with moss.

   _____

5. Leo trimmed the <u>garden</u> hedge.

   _____

6. Jessica and I watched a <u>cowboy</u> film.

   _____

7. <u>Musical</u> sounds could be heard in the hall.

   _____

8. <u>Dirt</u> roads began as the pavement ended.

   _____

9. The <u>Alaskan</u> salmon swam upstream.

   _____

10. The <u>street</u> sign had been knocked down.

   _____

CHAPTER 3

Self-Assessment

● Check *Always*, *Sometimes*, or *Never* to respond to each statement.

Writing	Always	Sometimes	Never
I can identify descriptive writing and its features.			
I understand how to effectively organize a descriptive paragraph.			
I use sensory language to create vivid descriptions.			
I can correctly use words that are often misused.			
I can use a thesaurus to find synonyms.			
I include all the key features when I write a descriptive paragraph.			

Grammar	Always	Sometimes	Never
I can identify and use descriptive adjectives.			
I can identify and use definite and indefinite articles.			
I can identify and use numerical adjectives.			
I can identify and use adjectives as subject complements.			
I can correctly form and use comparative and superlative adjectives.			
I can identify and use the proper forms of *little, less, least, few, fewer,* and *fewest*.			
I can identify and use demonstrative adjectives.			
I can identify and use interrogative adjectives.			
I can identify and use indefinite adjectives.			
I can identify adjective phrases and use them to describe nouns in sentences.			

● **Write the most useful thing you learned in this chapter.**

_____

_____

CHAPTER 4

Principal Parts of Verbs, Verb Phrases

- **Underline the verb or verb phrase in each sentence. Write *present, past, past participle,* or *present participle* to identify the principal part of each main verb.**

1. I talked with Param about our vacation.   _____

2. The actors are rehearsing three times a week.   _____

3. Several geese swim in the pond.   _____

4. Ted and René have written many poems.   _____

5. They yelled loudly during the game.   _____

6. The pilot has flown around the world before.   _____

7. Yesterday I read my poem in front of the class.   _____

8. The teacher had spoken to us about the problem.   _____

9. We can watch the parade from here.   _____

10. The plumber is fixing the drain now.   _____

11. My father drives a bus for the city.   _____

12. I should have finished the assignment last night.   _____

- **Now go back and circle auxiliary verbs in seven sentences.**

CHAPTER 4

Regular and Irregular Verbs

● **Write the past participle form of each verb in parentheses.**

1. All of the birds have _____ (fly) south for the winter.

2. The thorns had _____ (tear) a hole in my shirt.

3. Several plates were _____ (break) when the box fell.

4. I have already _____ (ring) the doorbell three times.

5. The contestants have _____ (wear) the same clothes for a week.

6. Mr. Whittel had _____ (write) a letter of recommendation for me.

● **Write the past form of each verb in parentheses.**

7. My aunt _____ (knit) me a scarf for my last birthday.

8. My family _____ (live) on Elm Street for five years.

9. The wet clothes _____ (dry) on the clothesline.

10. Sal's sister _____ (borrow) money from him last week.

11. Kelly _____ (bring) cheese and pretzels to the party.

12. I _____ (know) all the answers on yesterday's test.

CHAPTER 4
What Makes Good Persuasive Writing?

- **Under each heading, circle the letters of the *two* statements that best describe that feature of persuasive writing.**

    1. Feature: Introduction

        a. Let readers know your position on an issue.

        b. Briefly state the main reasons for your position.

        c. Give detailed facts that support your position.

    2. Feature: Audience

        a. Be brief because your audience may already know all the facts.

        b. Appeal to the emotions of those who support your position.

        c. Use solid facts and logic to persuade those who may not agree with you.

    3. Feature: Body

        a. State arguments that support your opinion.

        b. Give personal information about yourself.

        c. Provide rebuttals to arguments against your position.

    4. Feature: Conclusion

        a. Briefly summarize the most important arguments.

        b. Include additional facts that you may not have previously stated.

        c. Restate your opinion in a positive, assertive manner.

- **Read each sentence from a persuasive letter to a school newspaper. Write *I* (introduction), *B* (body), or *C* (conclusion) to identify where you would place each sentence in the letter.**

    5. It is important to remember that these machines bring in money that is used to support many school programs. _____

    6. I am writing this letter to explain why the school should keep soda machines on our campus. _____

    7. In closing, I would like to remind the administration of the financial support the soda machines provide during a time when our school may be forced to cancel some programs because of budget cuts. _____

    8. Some people might argue that the machines should be removed because spilled soda and discarded cans create a mess on our campus. _____

4 Troublesome Verbs

● **Circle the letter under the verb that correctly completes each sentence. If your answers are correct, the letters vertically will spell the answer to the riddle below.**

1. I like to _____ in the hammock to relax.	lie I	lay A
2. The sun _____ in the east.	rises N	raises T
3. Please _____ the times for 15 minutes.	sit T	set A
4. Smoke _____ from the factories.	rose M	raised H
5. Will you _____ me borrow that book?	left E	let U
6. Lawrence _____ himself the Greek alphabet.	learned M	taught S
7. Please _____ in the chair by the window.	sit H	set T
8. The students _____ their hands to answer the question.	raised R	rose H
9. The class _____ about the Great Wall of China.	learned O	taught A
10. Did you _____ your keys on the table?	let T	leave O
11. Sarah _____ the shirt on the bed.	lied D	laid M

Where do Iditarod racers keep their sled dogs?

Answer: ___ ___   ___   ___ ___ ___ ___ ___ ___ ___   ___
         1   2   3   4   5   6   7   8   9 10 11

CHAPTER 4

Transitive Verbs

● **Circle the transitive verb in each sentence. Then write the doer and the receiver of the verb's action.**

1. Each student brought a sack lunch.

   Doer: _____   **Receiver:** _____

2. Mr. Wilkins received a check in the mail.

   Doer: _____   **Receiver:** _____

3. Dory reads several pages every night.

   Doer: _____   **Receiver:** _____

4. I tore my shirt on the nail.

   Doer: _____   **Receiver:** _____

5. The teacher wrote two sentences on the board.

   Doer: _____   **Receiver:** _____

6. Mrs. Lopez teaches ballet at the community center.

   Doer: _____   **Receiver:** _____

7. After the concert we ate dinner at the café.

   Doer: _____   **Receiver:** _____

8. The birds preened their feathers in the warm sunshine.

   Doer: _____   **Receiver:** _____

9. The coach ordered new jerseys.

   Doer: _____   **Receiver:** _____

10. She types 60 words in a minute's time.

    Doer: _____   **Receiver:** _____

CHAPTER 4

Fact and Opinion

● **Identify each statement by writing** *fact* **or** *opinion*.

1. Our teacher, Ms. March, always provides great help. _____

2. Half of the students brought in art supplies and paint. _____

3. The delayed construction began last week. _____

4. A piece of fruit has fewer calories than a candy bar. _____

5. That book is definitely not worth the cost. _____

6. We traveled the greatest number of miles on Tuesday. _____

7. Turning in late work is the worst thing you can do. _____

8. The best course of action is to be patient and wait. _____

● **Write** *bandwagon, testimonial, loaded words,* **or** *vague generality* **to identify the propaganda technique used in each example.**

9. Be a part of the "in" crowd. Buy Fizzy Cola. _____

10. Taylor Hudson's outrageous views prove he is a political extremist. _____

11. Put a spring in your step with revitalizing New Day vitamins. _____

12. John Millionaire will buy an automobile only from Rex Company! _____

● **Many persuasive writers share facts and opinions as cause and effect statements. On a separate sheet of paper, copy a blank Cause and Effect Chart as shown on page 140. Complete the chart with a factual effect of your choice and an opinion for each "cause box" on the chart.**

Intransitive Verbs

• **Each pair of sentences includes the same verb. Circle the letter of the sentence that includes an intransitive verb.**

1. a. Katarina whistled a tune quite loudly.

   b. The wind whistled through the hole in the window.

2. a. We meet our deadlines every month.

   b. The scouts meet in the gym weekly.

3. a. A small rubber ball bounced down the steps.

   b. The child bounced the ball over the fence.

4. a. My dad sings in the shower every morning.

   b. Sometimes Leslie sings duets with her sister.

5. a. We ate until we were too full to move.

   b. The children ate the juicy watermelon on the back porch.

• **Write two sentences for each verb. Make the verb transitive in the first sentence. Make the verb intransitive in the second sentence.**

6. tapped

   _____

   _____

7. runs

   _____

   _____

8. studied

   _____

   _____

CHAPTER

4 Linking Verbs

● **Underline the verb in each sentence. Determine whether it is a transitive verb, an intransitive verb, or a linking verb, and circle the corresponding letter.**

1. I felt queasy after the long car ride.
   - f. transitive
   - s. intransitive
   - t. linking

2. Bacteria thrive in warm temperatures.
   - e. transitive
   - w. intransitive
   - i. linking

3. Mario ate the last apple.
   - o. transitive
   - w. intransitive
   - x. linking

4. This ornament came from China.
   - c. transitive
   - t. intransitive
   - d. linking

5. The paint looks dry.
   - r. transitive
   - h. intransitive
   - i. linking

6. That dog seems friendly.
   - i. transitive
   - m. intransitive
   - r. linking

7. The soccer players kicked the ball.
   - e. transitive
   - a. intransitive
   - n. linking

8. The two women at the table are twins.
   - a. transitive
   - l. intransitive
   - d. linking

● **Now write the circled letters on the lines. If your answers are correct, you will reveal the answer to the riddle.**

Why did the bicycle keep falling over?

Answer: because it was ___ ___ ___   ___ ___ ___ ___ ___
                        1   2   3   4   5   6   7   8

CHAPTER

4

Outline

● **Read each outline segment for a persuasive paragraph. Cross out the item that does not support the main topic. Choose an item from the phrase box below to replace it, and write it on the line.**

1. I. Michael James a Great Choice for Class Treasurer

    A. Collected money for 5th-grade field trip

    B. Takes his responsibilities seriously

    C. Earns good grades in his math classes

    D. Has two brothers and a sister

    _____

2. I. How to Be a Good Reader

    A. Read every day

    B. Use free library card

    C. Read a variety of material on different subjects

    D. Summarize the main ideas as you read

    _____

3. I. Be Prepared for an Earthquake

    A. Have a supply of nonperishable food

    B. Store drinking water in a protected space

    C. Can occur at any time

    D. Put together a first-aid kit

    _____

Replacements

Buy flashlights and extra batteries

Ask questions about what you read

Has served on the fund-raising committee

Occur at fault lines

Enjoy good TV shows

Plays baseball well

CHAPTER

4

Simple Tenses

● **Underline the verb or verb phrase in each sentence. Write *present*, *past*, or *future* to identify its tense.**

1. Blue-rayed limpets often graze on kelp.   _____

2. The small crab flattened its body against the rocks.   _____

3. A turtle will hatch from the buried egg.   _____

4. The gnarled branches bent in the strong winds.   _____

5. After a dive the cormorant dries its wings in the sun.   _____

6. The seaside provided a place of respite on hot days.   _____

7. Seashells will litter the sandy shore.   _____

8. I taste the salt in the sea spray.   _____

9. My sister shows me a beautiful whelk shell.   _____

10. We slept on the long drive home.   _____

● **Write a sentence for each verb in the tense indicated.**

11. go (past tense)

_____

12. continue (future tense)

_____

13. study (present tense)

_____

14. cry (past tense)

_____

CHAPTER
4

Progressive Tenses

● **Complete each sentence with the verb in parentheses in the tense indicated.**

1. Martin _____ a letter of application.   (*write:* present progressive)

2. The new family _____ into their house
   tomorrow.   (*move:* future progressive)

3. Several students _____ papers on the shelf.   (*stack:* present progressive)

4. The teacher _____ a lesson on simple
   machines.   (*plan:* past progressive)

5. Amir _____ how to scuba dive.   (*learn:* future progressive)

6. The baby _____ before he fell asleep.   (*cry:* past progressive)

7. I _____ to the beach Saturday.   (*drive:* future progressive)

8. We _____ a snack for the group.   (*prepare:* present progressive)

9. The big dog _____ under my desk this
   morning.   (*sleep:* past progressive)

10. The children _____ a mural for the hallway.   (*create:* past progressive)

● **Write two sentences for each verb. Use the present progressive
tense in the first sentence and the past progressive tense in
the second sentence.**

11. arrive

present progressive: _____

past progressive: _____

12. select

present progressive: _____

past progressive: _____

CHAPTER

4 Prefixes

● **Read the paragraph. Circle six words that include a prefix.**

     Pat was uncomfortable. She did not know a single person at the celebration. Then Pat turned as someone called her name. The young man was unfamiliar, and yet she seemed to recall meeting him before. "Impossible!" the man said. "Pat, I'm Jimmy!" Then Pat realized that he was a former neighbor. Jimmy had been a preteen the last time she had seen him. As Jimmy reunited her with his family, Pat thought that her day might turn out to be an interesting one after all.

● **Choose two of the words that you circled above. Use the word analysis charts below to analyze the meaning of the words. For an example of a word analysis chart, see page 138.**

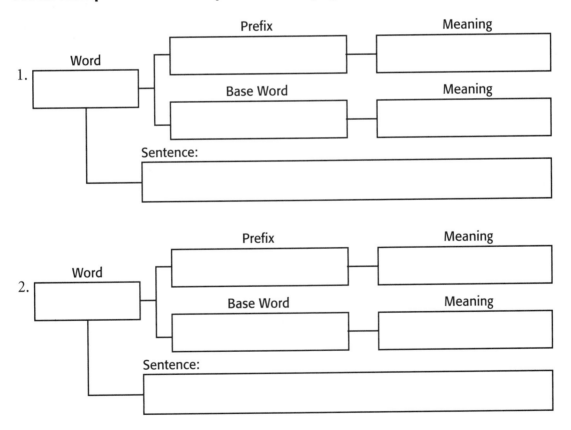

CHAPTER 4

Perfect Tenses

● **Underline the perfect tense verb in each sentence. Then write each verb in the correct column in the chart.**

1. Milos had saved the document on his computer.

2. He had attempted to swim across the Rio Grande last year.

3. The council members have notified Ms. Ropel of their decision.

4. I have read the last chapter of the book.

5. My aunt has replaced the old towels with new ones.

6. Dad had left dinner in the oven for us.

7. The large ship had run aground during the night.

8. My sister and I have saved enough money for a gift.

9. The baseball player has hit the winning homerun.

10. I had remembered my homework just in time.

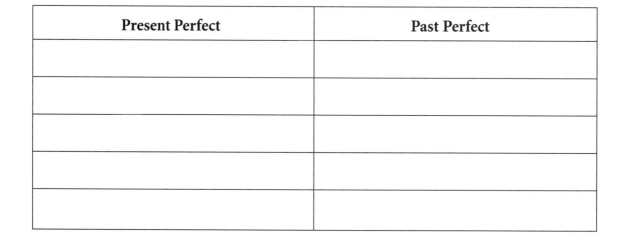

Present Perfect	Past Perfect

CHAPTER 4

Agreement of Subject and Verb

● **Underline the subject in each sentence. Then circle the correct singular or plural verb.**

1. There (is are) a banana on the counter.

2. I (doesn't don't) think I've read that book before.

3. Everybody (hope hopes) it will be sunny on Saturday.

4. The fish (is are) all in one corner of the aquarium.

5. Each of them (require requires) an application form.

6. No one (know knows) the answer to that question.

7. There (was were) hundreds of bats nesting in the cave.

8. You and I (play plays) on the same team.

9. My mother and Ian (like likes) to go fishing.

10. If Mia (don't doesn't) hurry, we'll have to leave without her.

● **Now find the verbs you circled above in the following word search. The words can be horizontal, vertical, or diagonal.**

W	A	H	E	Y	D	O	V	A	R	E	N	R	T	B	Y	A	O	G
U	G	R	T	E	D	E	N	L	L	E	M	D	E	I	D	W	U	H
A	E	T	R	E	Q	U	I	R	E	S	Y	K	O	U	S	A	A	N
W	T	R	L	G	N	L	P	T	S	U	X	N	Q	L	F	X	U	I
A	T	D	H	M	T	E	L	T	C	E	J	O	R	B	I	M	E	B
O	H	O	P	E	S	U	A	N	F	T	O	W	X	J	T	K	U	B
O	H	N	M	T	P	D	Y	O	D	O	E	S	N	T	V	E	E	O
I	B	T	A	O	X	A	S	B	Z	B	E	L	H	A	T	R	A	S

CHAPTER
4

Expanded Sentences

● **Add an appropriate prepositional phrase, adjective, or adverb to each sentence to make it more interesting.**

1. A _____ dog paced _____ .

2. The _____ woman read _____ .

3. _____ firefighters were talking _____ .

4. These _____ puppies are growing _____ .

5. The _____ actor gestured _____ .

6. _____ people cheered _____ .

7. That _____ horse jumped _____ .

8. _____ clouds floated _____ .

9. The _____ child realized _____ .

10. The _____ man slept _____ .

● **Write a simple sentence about each topic. Then trade papers with a partner. Add prepositional phrases, adjectives, and adverbs to expand your partner's sentences and make them more interesting.**

11. sports car _____

Expanded sentence: _____

12. teacher _____

Expanded sentence: _____

13. lunch _____

Expanded sentence: _____

14. goldfish _____

Expanded sentence: _____

CHAPTER 4

Active and Passive Voice

● **Underline the verb or verb phrase in each sentence. Identify the voice of each one by writing *active* or *passive*.**

1. The field trip was arranged by my homeroom teacher. _____

2. The hikers tracked muddy footprints throughout the house. _____

3. My dog chased a tennis ball across the grass. _____

4. The project was completed by a team of experts. _____

5. Many attempts were made by the opposing team. _____

6. Lauren and Sergei purchased tickets for the play. _____

7. My new magazine contained many creative ideas. _____

8. Every year many classes are attended by adults. _____

9. Keiko and Kelly rearranged the mess of papers. _____

10. The art supplies were placed into boxes by the two students. _____

● **Underline the verb phrase and circle the subject in each sentence. Then rewrite the sentence so the verb is in the active voice. The first one is done for you.**

11. A sculpture <u>was created</u> by the students for the art exhibit.

    The students created a sculpture for the art exhibit._____

12. A game of tag was played by the children.

    _____

13. An original story was read aloud by me.

    _____

14. Energy for plants is provided by the sun.

    _____

15. The drain was unclogged by the plumber this morning.

    _____

Name _____ Date _____

Self-Assessment

● Check *Always*, *Sometimes,* or *Never* to respond to each statement.

Writing	Always	Sometimes	Never
I can identify persuasive writing and its features.			
I can distinguish facts from opinions.			
I can organize my writing with an outline.			
I can identify and use words that include prefixes.			
I use prepositional phrases, adjectives, and adverbs to expand sentences and make them more interesting.			
I include all the key features when I write a persuasive paragraph.			

Grammar	Always	Sometimes	Never
I can identify and use the principal parts of verbs.			
I can identify and use verb phrases.			
I can identify and use regular and irregular forms of verbs.			
I can identify troublesome verbs and use them correctly.			
I can identify transitive and intransitive verbs and use them correctly.			
I can identify and use linking verbs.			
I can identify and use simple verb tenses.			
I can identify progressive verb tenses and use them correctly.			
I can identify perfect verb tenses and use them correctly.			
I can identify and use verbs so that they agree with their subjects in person and number.			
I can identify and use active and passive verbs.			

● **Write the most helpful thing you learned in this chapter.**

_____

_____

CHAPTER 5

Indicative Mood

● **Underline the verb or verb phrase in each sentence. Rewrite each sentence, adding a question mark or a period as necessary.**

1. Teresa studies every night for the upcoming test

   _____

2. Did Martin remind the class about their permission slips

   _____

3. Before the concert, where will you park the car

   _____

4. The trees were planted by several people

   _____

5. The museum displayed the new artist's painting

   _____

6. Will you help me with this project

   _____

● **Use each of the following verbs to write a sentence in the indicative mood. Use the verb tense given in parentheses.**

7. resolve (simple past) _____

   _____

8. construct (simple present) _____

   _____

9. aim (present progressive) _____

   _____

10. write (past perfect) _____

   _____

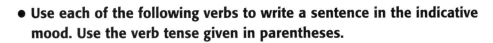

CHAPTER 5

Emphatic Form of the Indicative Mood

- **Underline the verb phrase used in the emphatic form of the indicative mood in each sentence. Write *past* or *present* to identify the verb tense.**

    1. I do swim a lot on warm days.   _____

    2. The sun does burn skin more easily at midday.   _____

    3. Marco did forget to bring the money for his books.   _____

    4. We did agree that this was the best decision.   _____

    5. The flowers did bloom earlier this year than last year. _____

    6. You do remember how to get there, don't you?   _____

    7. The dog does bark every time a stranger passes by.   _____

    8. That tree did topple during the storm.   _____

- **Rewrite each sentence using *do*, *does*, or *did* to change the underlined verb to the emphatic form in the same tense as the underlined verb.**

    9. This new car <u>resembles</u> last year's model.

    _____

    10. Last week the children <u>discovered</u> a new mountain trail.

    _____

    11. My science project <u>took</u> a lot of time.

    _____

    12. I <u>need</u> more time for this assignment.

    _____

CHAPTER 5

What Makes a Good Expository Article?

● **Read each statement. Circle *T* if the statement is true or *F* if it is false. Then rewrite each false statement to make it true.**

1. Expository writing is intended to inform you about a specific topic.   T   F

_____

2. Expository writing includes both factual and made-up details.   T   F

_____

3. Many newspaper articles are examples of expository writing.   T   F

_____

4. The body of an expository article can be presented only through comparing and contrasting or by a list of facts.   T   F

_____

_____

5. Expository writing for a newspaper addresses the *who, what, where,* and *how many* early in a composition.   T   F

_____

_____

6. Reporters often gather information for newspaper articles by talking to people who witnessed the event to be covered.   T   F

_____

_____

7. In the conclusion, introduce details that you forgot to include in the body paragraphs.   T   F

_____

8. A "lead" acts as a catchy beginning to attract a reader's attention.   T   F

_____

CHAPTER
5

Imperative Mood

● **Underline the verb or verb phrase in each sentence. Write *imperative* if the sentence is written in the imperative mood. Write *no* if it is not.**

1. Finish your work before the end of the day.   _____

2. The tour guide explained the newest exhibit.   _____

3. Please remove your dirty shoes from the couch.   _____

4. Find the directions to this game for me.   _____

5. Maddy's parents told everyone about the new rules.   _____

6. Write your name at the top of the paper.   _____

7. Please set these flower pots in front of the door.   _____

8. You should watch for fly balls!   _____

● **Rewrite each of the sentences above that is *not* imperative. Rewrite it as an imperative sentence.**

9. _____

_____

_____

10. _____

_____

_____

11. _____

_____

_____

CHAPTER 5

Subjunctive Mood

- **Write the letter that identifies how the subjunctive form is used in each sentence. Underline the verb form in each part of the sentence.**

    a. express a wish   b. contrary to fact   c. after verb of command

1. If the child were not so shy, he would have joined the game.   _____

2. She wishes she were able to compete in the track meet.   _____

3. If Min were happy, she'd have a big smile on her face.   _____

4. I wish that my team were the tournament champions.   _____

5. If I were my brother, I would want a new car.   _____

6. My mother suggested that I be more careful next time.   _____

7. The principal insisted that we be quiet in the library.   _____

8. If you were the winner, you'd want the prize.   _____

- **Circle the correct form of the verb for the subjunctive. Complete each sentence with your own idea.**

9. If you (was   were) living at the beach, you could _____.

10. His father suggested that he (be   was) _____.

11. I wish I (were   was) _____.

12. I wish we (was   were) _____.

13. If I (was   were) richer, I'd _____.

14. The students demanded that the teachers (were   be) _____.

CHAPTER 5 Interviewing

● **Read each sentence that might be used in an interview about an upcoming event. Write *who, what, where, when,* or *why* to classify each type of sentence.**

1. In what city will the Garlic Festival be held? _____

2. During what time of the year does the city plan to hold the concert? _____

3. Which celebrities do you expect will attend the golf tournament? _____

4. Can you explain why the event has been moved to a bigger site? _____

5. Tell me your ideas for this year's fundraiser. _____

● **Read the questions for an interview with the organizer of an upcoming community soccer camp. Tell why each is inappropriate or unnecessary for the interview. Write a new question to replace each one.**

6. I think soccer is boring, so why do you think this camp is necessary?

_____

_____

7. How long can you afford to run this soccer camp?

_____

_____

8. What other sports do you think would benefit from a project like this?

_____

_____

9. What hobbies do you have?

_____

_____

5 Modal Auxiliaries

● **Complete each sentence with the meaning indicated in parentheses. Use a modal auxiliary from the word box.**

may	might	could	can	must	should	would

1. The author _____ sign copies of her book this afternoon. (possibility)

2. You _____ help me put away these books. (ability)

3. Sarah _____ borrow my backpack if she needs it. (permission)

4. Hasani _____ need to fill out this form in order to join the club. (willingness)

5. _____ you like to explain your answer to the class? (willingness)

6. The money _____ be available before we can purchase our supplies. (necessity)

7. Your parents _____ provide the materials you will need. (ability)

8. You _____ use this coupon to get a free ticket. (permission)

9. The dance _____ be over by 9:00 this evening. (necessity)

10. My mom _____ want to drive us herself. (possibility)

● **With a partner find in a newspaper two examples of sentences that use modal auxiliaries. Write the sentences.**

11. _____

12. _____

CHAPTER 5
Adverbs of Time, Place, and Manner

● **Underline the adverb in each sentence. Circle the verb it modifies. Then circle the letter that identifies whether the adverb shows time, place, or manner.**

1. My family recently traveled to the coast on vacation.
   - t. time
   - s. place
   - r. manner

2. Amber won the debate because she spoke clearly.
   - i. time
   - e. place
   - a. manner

3. The soldiers saluted their commander precisely.
   - p. time
   - t. place
   - l. manner

4. We seldom see black bears in this part of the state.
   - o. time
   - a. place
   - s. manner

5. Luis, put the box here on the table.
   - f. time
   - n. place
   - g. manner

6. The bus moved forward when the stoplight changed.
   - s. time
   - t. place
   - m. manner

7. The people quickly gathered their belongings.
   - b. time
   - l. place
   - e. manner

8. Damon usually jogs at the school track.
   - d. time
   - n. place
   - s. manner

● **Write the circled letters in order on the lines. If your answers are correct, you will reveal the answer to the riddle.**

What would you call a hawk that could play the piano with its feet?

Answer: Very ___ ___ ___ ___ ___ - ___ ___ ___
                  1   2   3   4   5   6   7   8

CHAPTER 5

Using Quotations

● **Read each group of sentences. Choose the quotation from the box that matches the sentences and write the quotation after them. For each quotation, replace the word *said* with a more interesting verb.**

> A. It was he who said, "An ounce of prevention is worth a pound of cure."
>
> B. "This wariness is what makes them such good watch dogs," the trainer said.
>
> C. "How can you not fall in love with California?" he said.
>
> D. "If we are very still," the ornithologist said, "the birds will relax and forget we are here."
>
> E. "The water is very salty," she said, "and these structures form as the water evaporates."

1. Great tufa towers rose up over the still waters of the lake. Geologist Karen Thomas pointed out the tallest of the formations. _____

   _____

2. As an author and philosopher, Benjamin Franklin coined many popular sayings we know today. _____

   _____

3. We learned that when the cormorants feel protected and safe from predators, they spread their wings wide. This behavior dries their feathers and allows them to collect the sun's radiant warmth. _____

   _____

4. Our tour guide paused on the trail and pointed out the distant view. Over an expanse of blue water, the Golden Gate Bridge glowed in the morning sun. _____

   _____

5. The puppies tumbled and wrestled with one another. A sudden noise made them stop at once, suddenly at full attention. _____

   _____

CHAPTER 5

Adverbs of Degree, Affirmation, and Negation

- **Underline the adverb in each sentence. Then write *degree, affirmation,* or *negation* to identify how the adverb is used.**

1. This rainstorm was undoubtedly worse than Monday's storm. _____

2. We had scarcely begun when our time was up. _____

3. That version of the book is much better. _____

4. Logan would indeed prefer to lead the way. _____

5. The sea is exceedingly rough today. _____

6. Jorge never takes the long way home. _____

7. Yes, the garden was watered this morning. _____

8. The tickets are no longer for sale. _____

9. The students' test results were quite impressive. _____

10. She could not find her homework in the stack of papers. _____

11. Mr. Rhodes found the directions rather difficult to follow. _____

12. We all agreed that Elisa's performance had improved dramatically. _____

- **Write three original sentences, one that uses an adverb of degree, one that uses an adverb of affirmation, and one that uses an adverb of negation.**

13. _____

_____

14. _____

_____

15. _____

_____

CHAPTER 5

Comparative and Superlative Adverbs

● **Write the comparative and superlative form of each adverb.**

	Comparative	Superlative
1. well	_____	_____
2. sincerely	_____	_____
3. little	_____	_____
4. late	_____	_____
5. much	_____	_____

● **Write the correct comparative or superlative form of the adverb in parentheses to complete each sentence.**

6. The winner is the one who stays _____ on the bronco. (long)

7. Marcie reads _____ than I do. (well)

8. The other player threw the javelin _____ than his opponent. (far)

9. The shy boy speaks _____ than his sister. (quietly)

10. Of all the routes he takes, Mr. Huang finishes this one _____. (rapidly)

● **Write a sentence that includes the comparative or the superlative form of each of the following adverbs.**

11. carefully

_____

12. hastily

_____

CHAPTER 5

Taking Notes

● **Read the notes a student recorded about Rio de Janeiro. Then answer the questions in complete sentences.**

	Rio de Janeiro
	means "river of January" because it was discovered on 1/1/1502
	Geography
○	city in SE Brazil
	2nd biggest city
	between mtns & Atlantic O.
	tropical climate: high 95°F, low 68°F
	Culture
	ethnic makeup: African, European, Native American
	major industry: tourism & entertain.
	many great sandy beaches, universities, museums, churches
	Carnival: festival in late Feb/early Mar

1. How did Rio de Janeiro get its name? _____

_____

2. Where is this city located? _____

_____

3. What is there to do if you visit Rio de Janeiro? _____

_____

● **Make a KWL chart about Carnival. Write when and where Carnival happens in the first column. Write three questions you have about Carnival in the second column. Research the answers, and complete the last column.**

CHAPTER 5

Adverbs and Adjectives

● Circle the word that correctly completes each sentence. Write the number under the word in the box at the end of the sentence.

Start with	_____
Add	_____
Add	_____
Subtract	_____
Subtract	_____
Add	_____
Subtract	_____
Subtract	_____
Subtract	_____
Add	_____
Subtract	_____
Add	_____

1. Those roses smell (sweet   sweetly) but have thorns.
                          8   7

2. Nightingales sing (soft   softly) from the boughs of the trees.
                     2   4

3. Carmen paddled (smooth   smoothly) against the strong current.
                  9   7

4. After sitting in the sun, Leo felt (warm   warmly).
                               8   9

5. I'll sleep (good   well) after working in the yard all day.
               1   3

6. Cows chew their cud (slow   slowly).
                  4   9

7. These lemon drops really do taste (sour   sourly).
                       2   4

8. The train whistle blew (loud   loudly) to alert the passengers.
                 3   2

9. A kudzu vine will grow (quick   quickly).
                  8   9

10. The ball bounced (aimless   aimlessly) down the hill.
                6   8

11. Lamb's wool feels (soft   softly).
             3   5

12. We closed the office door (quiet   quietly) behind us.
                8   6

● Now follow the directions to add and subtract the numbers in order to reveal the answer to the trivia question.

How many players are on a rugby team? _____

CHAPTER 5

Negative Words

● **Circle the word that correctly completes each sentence.**

1. We didn't find (no   any) shells at the beach.

2. Haven't you (ever   never) missed a day of school?

3. Tony had (no   any) excuse for being so late.

4. Mr. Eldin hasn't (no   any) time to help us with the project.

5. A two-year-old has (no   any) use for an encyclopedia.

6. I (ever   never) make the same mistake twice.

● **Rewrite the sentences below to correct any errors. If a sentence is correct as is, write *Correct*.**

7. The detectives could not find no clues.

_____

8. Maria couldn't never remember to close the door.

_____

9. Jenell didn't have any time to go to the post office.

_____

10. I haven't no money to lend you.

_____

11. No one never goes there.

_____

12. I never bought any books for my class.

_____

Homophones

● **Use a homophone pair from the word box to complete each sentence.**

hoarse, horse	piece, peace	night, knight	new, knew
bored, board	won, one	your, you're	seas, seize

1. To keep the _____, the babysitter offered each child a _____ of candy.

2. We cheered so loudly each time a _____ cleared a jump that our voices became _____.

3. _____ so helpful to loan me _____ class notes.

4. Only _____ person _____ the grand prize.

5. The pirates sailed the _____ in search of treasure they could _____.

6. The shadowy figure of the _____ galloped off into the dark _____.

7. Because he was _____, Leo spent an hour pounding nails into a _____.

8. No one _____ where Lynn left her _____ jacket.

● **Look at the sample word analysis chart on page 138. Copy two blank charts on a separate sheet of paper. Complete the charts using the homophones *seas* and *seize*.**

CHAPTER 5

Adverb Phrases and Clauses

● **Underline the adverb phrase in each sentence. Circle the verb it describes.**

   1. Our school flag flies above the stadium.

   2. The children skated across the ice-covered pond.

   3. The new play was performed in the school auditorium.

   4. Their new puppy rolled down the grassy slope.

   5. The statue of the president was designed with great care.

● **Underline the adverb clause in each sentence.**

   6. Because our class read the most books, we earned a lunchtime pizza party.

   7. I cheered when my sister scored the winning goal.

   8. We hid the presents where Hector would not find them.

   9. After the teacher corrects the final exams, she will post our semester grades.

  10. I will prepare the turkey while you mash the potatoes.

● **Complete each sentence with an adverb phrase. Circle the verb your adverb phrase describes.**

  11. We watched the snake slither _____.

  12. The thunderous waves crashed _____.

  13. My new poster hangs _____.

  14. The small child walked _____.

Name _____   Date _____

Self-Assessment

● Check *Always, Sometimes,* or *Never* to respond to each statement.

Writing	Always	Sometimes	Never
I can identify expository writing and its features.			
I understand how to conduct an interview.			
I understand how to use quotations.			
I use shortcuts when I take notes.			
I can identify homophones and use them correctly.			
I include all the key features when I write an expository article.			

Grammar	Always	Sometimes	Never
I can identify and use verbs in the indicative mood.			
I can identify and use verbs in the emphatic form of the indicative mood.			
I can identify and use verbs in the imperative mood.			
I can identify and use verbs in the subjunctive mood.			
I can identify and use modal auxiliaries.			
I can identify and use adverbs to show time, place, and manner.			
I can identify and use adverbs to show degree, affirmation, and negation.			
I can form and use comparative and superlative adverbs.			
I can recognize the difference between adjectives and adverbs and use them correctly.			
I can identify and use negative adverbs and adjectives and correct double negatives in sentences.			
I can identify and use adverb phrases and adverb clauses.			

● **How would you teach others what you learned in this chapter?**

_____

_____

CHAPTER

6 Subjects and Predicates

- **Underline the complete subject in each sentence. Circle the simple subject.**

  1. Kiana wondered how the story would end.

  2. A few falcons made a nest on top of the old building.

  3. The scientist carefully poured the chemicals into the beaker.

  4. Dandelion seeds floated through the air.

  5. New York City is an exciting place to visit.

  6. The scruffy, white dog wagged its tail enthusiastically.

- **Underline the complete predicate in each sentence. Circle the simple predicate.**

  7. A hazy, blue mist rose over the lake.

  8. Mom and Dad will bring the ice chest and the umbrella.

  9. The exhausted hikers rested by the river.

  10. Our new boat is blue and white.

  11. My older brother might buy me a guitar.

  12. The ducklings are swimming across the pond.

- **Write a complete predicate to finish each sentence. Circle the simple predicate.**

  13. The eerie howling in the distance _____.

  14. A two-million-dollar prize _____.

  15. The multicolored hot-air balloons _____.

CHAPTER

6 Natural and Inverted Order

• **Circle the letter under *Natural* or *Inverted* to identify the order of each sentence. Then write the circled letters on the lines below to answer the riddle.**

	Natural	Inverted
1. Along the rocks lay hundreds of mussels and clams.	S	F
2. In the backyard were many children.	T	O
3. Several hundred people waited at the train depot.	U	R
4. In winter we enjoy sledding and skiing.	N	S
5. Outside the window sat a hungry bird.	I	D
6. A large billboard stood in the empty field.	P	S
7. Adam left his backpack in the grocery store.	A	E
8. Did you know the answer to that last question?	R	C
9. My little sister took the last piece of banana bread.	K	M
10. Over the city floated a striped balloon.	O	S

How are a playing card and a wolf alike?

Answer: They are both ___ ___ ___ ___ ___ in ___ ___ ___ ___ ___.
      1   2   3   4   5   6   7   8   9   10

• **Rewrite each sentence in inverted order.**

11. An abandoned car was near the playground.

_____

12. Most students are in which class?

_____

13. The sun emerged from behind the clouds.

_____

What Makes a Good Business Letter?

● **Read the business letter. Then answer the questions.**

Santa Maria Art League
602 First Street
Santa Maria, NV 84963

January 9, 20–

Mrs. Teresa Williams
Art Teacher
Roosevelt Middle School
737 Roosevelt Avenue
Santa Maria, NV 84960

Dear Mrs. Williams:

Thank you for your interest in our spring student art exhibit. I am happy to provide you with the information you requested.

The exhibition will be held March 25–30 of this year. In order for each student to be properly represented, please label each piece of artwork with the student's full name and age and the medium used. Encourage students to title their entries. All submissions should be received at the Art League by March 10.

I hope this information is helpful. Let me know if you need further details. We look forward to viewing the artwork submitted by your students.

Sincerely,

Mimi Gomez

Mimi Gomez, Art League President

1. What is the purpose of this business letter?

   _____

2. What are some of the details the letter provides?

   _____

   _____

3. What invitation to action does the sender give in the last paragraph?

   _____

4. Name the elements of this business letter that distinguish it from a personal one.

   _____

   _____

CHAPTER
6 Types of Sentences

● **Write *declarative, interrogative, imperative,* or *exclamatory* to identify each sentence. Add the correct end punctuation.**

1. Do you know what time the meeting starts   _____

2. Heavy, dark clouds filled the summer sky   _____

3. Hey, that looks like the winning ticket   _____

4. Put your backpack under the hallway table   _____

5. Have you seen my library book on the Civil War   _____

6. Please write your name on the first line   _____

7. That was the most exciting movie I have ever seen   _____

8. Can you give me directions to the nearest bookstore   _____

● **Think about something that happened to you over the weekend. Write what happened and be sure to include one example of each type of sentence.**

_____

_____

_____

_____

_____

_____

_____

_____

_____

CHAPTER 6
Simple and Compound Sentences

- **In each compound sentence, circle the simple subject and underline the simple predicate of each independent clause.**

    1. She smiled at the camera, so the photographer took the picture.

    2. I washed the dishes, and my sister dried them.

    3. Mrs. Wilkes rescues stray cats, but first she wins their trust.

    4. He is a popular artist, yet his paintings are inexpensive.

    5. Tai must arrive by nine o'clock, or the bus will leave without him.

    6. Jackson likes apples, but the fruit stand did not have any.

- **Write *simple* or *compound* to identify each sentence. Underline the two independent clauses in each compound sentence.**

    7. A warm, steaming cup of coffee sat on the kitchen counter.   _____

    8. I was already late for school, so I ran the entire way.   _____

    9. Geese migrate to the lake, and they nest there for
       the winter.   _____

    10. Both the football team and the soccer club sponsored
        the fundraiser.   _____

    11. The puppy chewed a hole in the sock, but it was an old
        one anyway.   _____

    12. Trisha cleaned and polished the new dining room table.   _____

CHAPTER 6

Audience, Tone, and Formal Language

● **Read each sentence from a business letter. Identify the problem with tone, lack of formal language, or lack of a strong, detailed idea. Then rewrite each sentence so that it is formal, polite, and professional.**

1. I would like to say, "Way to go," about the totally awesome scholarship award you received.

   Problem: _____

   Rewrite: _____

2. You must be crazy to think I would want to keep such a piece of junk as this handheld radio.

   Problem: _____

   Rewrite: _____

3. I'm writing to explain how you're to apply for a full refund.

   Problem: _____

   Rewrite: _____

4. I think that the new blond guy is a great addition to your afternoon program staff.

   Problem: _____

   Rewrite: _____

5. Wow, I am so totally impressed by your generosity I could scream!

   Problem: _____

   Rewrite: _____

6. I am a good worker who would be a good employee.

   Problem: _____

   Rewrite: _____

Punctuation of Compound Sentences

CHAPTER 6

- **Write *correct* if the compound sentence has been written and punctuated correctly. If it has not, write *incorrect* and rewrite the sentence.**

1. We often sail on the lake but we never fish there.
   _____
   _____

2. Run quickly or you will miss the bus.
   _____
   _____

3. I take violin lessons my sister takes karate lessons.
   _____
   _____

4. The sky turned black yet we remained on the playing field.
   _____
   _____

5. Maggie does not like spinach, nor does she like lima beans.
   _____
   _____

- **Rewrite each pair of simple sentences as a compound sentence.**

6. The race will be difficult.
   I run every day.
   _____

7. Anthony planned to attend the conference.
   He didn't have enough money.
   _____

8. I set my clothes by the warm fire.
   They dried quickly.
   _____

9. The cat cried constantly.
   Its dish was full of food.
   _____

CHAPTER 6

Prepositions and Prepositional Phrases

● **Underline the prepositional phrase in each sentence. Circle the object of the preposition.**

1. Two gray squirrels played under the apple tree.

2. In the winter our entire family skis.

3. The fly ball landed near my car.

4. Jamie took the last slice of cranberry bread.

5. Our vacation in Mexico was truly exciting.

● **Use a preposition from the box to complete each sentence. Then underline all the prepositional phrases.**

because of	toward	under	during
from	behind	with	for

6. _____ the rain we stayed under the canopy.

7. Keisha and the twins are coming _____ me to the store.

8. I took a pottery class _____ the spring semester at our college.

9. It rained continuously _____ six days.

10. José found the missing book _____ the stack of papers.

11. Please place the file for Williams _____ the one for Walters.

12. He received a birthday card _____ his grandmother.

13. The runners raced quickly _____ the finish line.

CHAPTER 6 Suffixes

● **Circle the word that correctly completes each sentence. Then identify the part of speech of the circled word.**

1. The teenager acted (childish   childishly) when his name was not announced.

2. Press the button to (activate   activist) the machine.   _____

3. The (manageable   manager) of the department store was quite helpful.   _____

4. The driver made a (skillful   skillfully) maneuver.   _____

5. We toured the (botanist   botanical) gardens when we were in Atlanta.   _____

6. The class was in (agreement   agreeable) about the choice for our motto.   _____

● **Complete the word analysis chart for the suffix *-ish*. Then, on a separate sheet of paper, complete another word analysis chart for a suffix of your choice: tell its meaning, name three words using the suffix, and provide a meaning for each word. For an example of a word analysis chart, see page 138.**

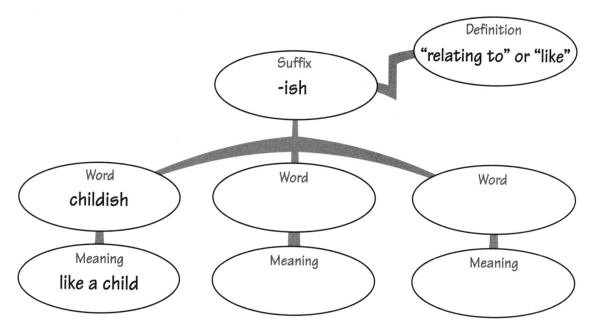

CHAPTER
6

Using Prepositions Correctly

● Circle the preposition that correctly completes each sentence. Then write a sentence that includes the other preposition. The first one has been done for you.

1. Our annual family reunion was (at) to) the park by the bay.

   We drove to the park for a picnic._____

2. Why don't you share the toys (between   among) the three of you?

   _____

3. The fly was stuck (between   among) the screen and the door.

   _____

4. Would you stand (beside   besides) me at the assembly?

   _____

5. Mekia and Miguel peered cautiously (in   into) the cave.

   _____

6. (Beside   Besides) apples, what is your favorite fruit?

   _____

7. The goats walked (at   to) the stream to drink.

   _____

8. Adriana wondered what was (in   into) the box.

   _____

9. We saw a small sea star (beside   besides) the rock.

   _____

10. The car is parked (between   among) the two buildings.

   _____

11. Mya said he was (at   to) the party last week.

   _____

CHAPTER 6 Prepositions and Adverbs

● **Circle the number at the end of each sentence to indicate if the underlined word is used as an adverb or as a preposition.**

	Adverb	Preposition
1. The teacher pointed <u>above</u>.	91.50	123.90
2. The temperature was three degrees <u>below</u> zero.	77.90	68.72
3. Weeds sprang <u>up</u> uncontrollably all over the yard.	27.98	43.42
4. Have you been to this doctor <u>before</u>?	100.00	150.01
5. We looked out at the valley <u>below</u>.	12.78	99.00
6. Birds of prey soared <u>over</u> the roofs.	100.77	111.23
7. The quarterback stood <u>outside</u> the huddle.	52.55	52.08
8. Jana wrote a paper <u>about</u> the first emperor of Rome.	200.40	22.10
9. The officer asked us to wait <u>outside</u>.	83.84	90.09
10. I barely finished my report <u>before</u> the deadline.	46.07	52.00
11. The boat sailed <u>up</u> the swiftly moving river.	10.98	11.65
12. The sun went <u>down</u>, leaving a glowing red sky.	53.10	63.32

● **Add the numbers you circled above to answer the question.**

A year on Earth is 365.26 days long. How many days is a year on Mars?

Answer: _____ Earth days

CHAPTER 6

Expanding Sentences

● **Underline the compound subject or predicate in each sentence. Write**
  subject **or** *predicate* **to identify the compound part.**

1. Football and baseball are my favorite sports.   _____

2. Sarah cracked and beat three eggs.   _____

3. Minneapolis and St. Paul are called the Twin Cities.   _____

4. My uncle composes and performs his own music.   _____

5. The photographer shoots and develops portraits.   _____

6. Mosquitoes and bees appear with the warm weather.   _____

● **Follow the directions to write a compound direct object or object of**
  the preposition to complete each sentence. The first one has been
  done for you.

7. On our vacation, we rented ___jet skis and kayaks___.
   (direct object)

8. The track team often runs _____.
   (object of a preposition)

9. During the concert, the musician played _____.
   (direct object)

10. From his coin jar, Luis counted only _____.
    (direct object)

11. The kittens were hiding _____.
    (object of a preposition)

12. After school, I take lessons _____.
    (object of a preposition)

CHAPTER 6 Adjective Phrases

● **Underline the adjective phrase in each sentence. Circle the noun that each phrase modifies.**

1. The walls of the castle were colorfully decorated.

2. This is the workshop of a silversmith.

3. The capital city of Nebraska is Lincoln.

4. Our seats for the concert were amazing.

5. The laughter of the amused crowd delighted the children.

6. The day before yesterday was my birthday.

7. Their new cabin by the lake has 10 rooms.

8. One extremely strong natural fiber is silk from spiders.

9. This store features seashells from the Pacific.

10. A leak in the pipe caused the damage.

● **Find the nouns you circled in the word search. Words can go across, down, or diagonally.**

```
N  S  E  W  O  R  K  S  H  O  P  S  T  O  Y  L
E  O  S  E  A  S  H  E  L  L  S  R  H  T  O  E
B  D  S  S  T  L  E  K  C  R  O  W  I  R  U  A
P  U  A  E  E  D  L  S  S  I  L  C  A  S  T  K
R  S  T  Y  R  I  R  S  L  A  U  G  H  T  E  R
A  T  P  I  S  D  A  X  V  C  A  B  I  N  E  R
S  H  S  E  A  T  S  R  M  S  M  I  T  T  H  Y
```

CHAPTER 6 Adverb Phrases

● **Underline the adverb phrase in each sentence. Circle the word it describes.**

1. The frightened child hid under the bed.

2. Some fans ran onto the field.

3. Our family portrait hangs above the fireplace.

4. Lacey and Cheryl study with their friends.

5. Dr. Mendez volunteers at the clinic.

6. The playful kitten crawled into the paper bag.

7. We walked across the bridge to get a better view.

8. Snowball hopped onto the box and ate the carrot.

● **Write a sentence that includes each adverb phrase.**

9. over each other

_____

_____

10. into the hole

_____

_____

11. with obvious glee

_____

_____

12. after her stunning performance

_____

_____

Mailing a Letter

CHAPTER 6

● **Study the envelope for a business letter. Identify six changes you could make to it.**

James Nichols
890 Alpha Boulevard
Kirkwood, Delaware 19708

Missus Patricia Williams
Spinning Wheels Bicycle Shop
19078 Lassen Pkwy, Building 7
Avalon, New Jersey 08202

---

1. _____ 2. _____

3. _____ 4. _____

5. _____ 6. _____

● **Write *true* or *false* for each statement about mailing a business letter. Rewrite each false statement so it is true.**

7. Fold a business letter into quarters before inserting it into an envelope.   _____

   _____

8. If you forget the postage, the post office will attach it for you.   _____

   _____

9. List any enclosures so the reader knows what to look for.   _____

   _____

10. Write business letters on $8\frac{1}{2}$" × 11" paper.   _____

   _____

11. Write out the state name when addressing the envelope.   _____

   _____

CHAPTER 6

Complex Sentences and Adverb Clauses

● **For each sentence underline the clause listed in parentheses.**

1. The volcano became a tourist attraction when it erupted.   (dependent)

2. The cat meowed loudly because it was his mealtime.   (independent)

3. After the rain had stopped, we resumed the ballgame.   (independent)

4. Although I was tired, I helped my sister with her homework.   (dependent)

5. Sam borrowed 20 dollars since he had spent his money.   (independent)

6. The mouse scurried under the log when it spotted the cat.   (dependent)

7. When the siren sounded, the children reacted with surprise.   (independent)

8. Because the power went out, we looked for the flashlights.   (dependent)

● **Underline the dependent adverb clause in each sentence.**

9. When Kelly heard the doorbell ring, she rushed to answer the door.

10. I will wash the car while my brother mows the lawn.

11. Please don't start the movie until I make the popcorn.

12. After the game ended, we went to Pizza Palace for dinner.

13. If Sheyna finishes her homework, she can go to the dance tonight.

14. Phong failed the test because he had not studied.

CHAPTER 6
Self-Assessment

- **Check *Always, Sometimes,* or *Never* to respond to each statement.**

Writing	Always	Sometimes	Never
I can identify a business letter and its features.			
I understand how to address my audience and use proper tone and language in a business letter.			
I can use suffixes to understand word meanings.			
I can expand sentences using compound subjects and predicates.			
I can address an envelope and fold a business letter.			
I include all the key features when I write a business letter.			

Grammar	Always	Sometimes	Never
I can identify and use subjects and predicates.			
I can identify and use natural and inverted order.			
I can identify and use declarative, interrogative, imperative, and exclamatory sentences.			
I can identify and use simple and compound sentences.			
I can correctly punctuate compound sentences.			
I can identify and use prepositions and prepositional phrases.			
I can use troublesome prepositions correctly.			
I can distinguish between words used as prepositions or as adverbs.			
I can identify and use adjective phrases.			
I can identify and use adverb phrases.			
I can identify and use adverb clauses.			

- **Write how what you learned in this chapter can help you communicate with others.**

_____

_____

CHAPTER
7

Conjunctions

● **Circle the coordinating conjunction in each sentence. Underline the words it connects and write *nouns, adjectives, adverbs, prepositional phrases,* or *independent clauses* to identify the words it connects.**

1. The bicycle and the car are in the garage. _____

2. Pete could not go to the game or to the picnic. _____

3. Reba or Amie will play first base during the game. _____

4. Brass is a mixture of copper and zinc. _____

5. Have you studied or played all afternoon? _____

6. Jay raises the flag, and Keesha takes it down. _____

7. Beth seems excited but nervous about her performance. _____

8. Would you like lemon or milk in your tea? _____

9. The students worked quickly yet quietly. _____

● **Write a sentence that contains a coordinating conjunction to connect each pair of words or phrases.**

10. in the closet, under the bed

_____

11. studied, practiced

_____

12. dangerous, important

_____

CHAPTER 7

Interjections

● **In the puzzle find and circle the eight words that are common interjections. Words can go across, down, or diagonally.**

Wow	Hooray	Oops	Aha
No	Hush	Hello	Ouch

A D H O O R A Y B M C Y A D S E

Q F G E Y M E I X S A Z H A O B

H N A Z L U S F P B X J A T U C

W S O S N L B O B J Q N X F C B

C O T P A X O M Z H U S H Q H D

Y A W C S T P A X Y P M N X E A

● **Now use the interjections you circled to complete the sentences. Then write the emotion or feeling you think each expresses.**

Emotion or Feeling

1. _____! I knew I could find where the prize was hidden. _____

2. _____! It is so good to see you. _____

3. _____! I smashed my finger when I moved the rock. _____

4. _____! I spilled the fruit juice all over the counter. _____

5. _____! We cannot hear what the speaker is saying. _____

6. _____! That is the most beautiful sunset ever! _____

7. _____! My parents decided on a vacation to Hawaii. _____

8. _____! That is not my mess in the living room. _____

CHAPTER 7
What Makes a Good Trickster Tale?

- **Circle the best answer to complete each statement about a trickster tale.**

  1. A trickster tale is a story that

     a. tells how a weak but clever character outwits a powerful rival.

     b. explains how a magician performs tricks.

     c. shows how a physically strong character can outwit a weaker character.

  2. A trickster tale

     a. has a beginning, a middle, and an end.

     b. is usually told in chronological order.

     c. includes both of the above.

  3. The beginning of a trickster tale

     a. usually gives away the ending.

     b. always gives factual information about the animals of the story.

     c. usually introduces the trickster, the victim, and the setting.

  4. The middle part of a trickster tale

     a. develops the plot in which the trickster tries to outwit a rival to achieve a goal.

     b. uses a pattern of events to tell the story backwards.

     c. never uses literary techniques like foreshadowing or dialog.

  5. A trickster tale ends when

     a. all of the characters in the story are introduced.

     b. the trickster's goal is achieved or its plan backfires.

     c. all of the goals from the beginning are restated.

- **Use the answers you marked above to analyze the features in a trickster tale of your choice. In what parts of the story can you find each characteristic? Share your findings with a classmate.**

CHAPTER 7

Periods

● **Add periods where needed in each sentence. Use proofreader's mark as shown here.** *Example:* **Mr⊙Koll lives next door** ⊙

1. Mrs Frisby, a field mouse, is a character in a book by Robert C O'Brien

2. The meeting is scheduled for 2:00 p m on Sat, Apr 4

3. Gen Amos M Pritchard and Lt Jorge T Garcia are military translators for the army

4. Mrs Roberta Byrd works at the Nimitz St office

5. I wrote a letter to the Business Machines Co to request a refund

6. Her address is 1414 E Lassen Ave in Cincinnati

7. The new instructor's name is Mr Lance K Brightman

8. On Nov 25 we will hold a meeting in Phoenix at 8:00

● **Write an abbreviation for each word.**

9. gallon _____   10. Highway _____

11. Wyoming _____   12. ounce _____

13. Senator _____   14. Arizona _____

15. milliliter _____   16. Boulevard _____

● **Find at least 10 abbreviations in a newspaper. On a separate sheet of paper, list the abbreviations and write what each one stands for.**

CHAPTER 7

Commas

● Add commas to the following sentences. Then write the letter of the comma rule that is illustrated by the sentence. Use proofreader's marks when marking corrections. *Example:* My favorite place⹁Lincoln Park Zoo⹁is open year-round.

> A. set off parts of dates, addresses, and places
>
> B. set off a nonrestrictive appositive
>
> C. separate items in a series
>
> D. set off a direct quotation
>
> E. separate clauses

1. Nina played volleyball tennis and soccer yesterday. _____

2. My parents were married on August 12 1988 in New York City. _____

3. It was too stormy for boating so we stayed inside. _____

4. A circus museum is located in Baraboo Wisconsin just south of the Wisconsin Dells. _____

5. The limerick a five-line poem is always humorous. _____

6. I visit El Dorado County California at least once each year. _____

7. "Tokyo is an important city in Japan" remarked the teacher. _____

8. The heart a vital organ of the body needs exercise. _____

9. Marco my brother will be attending the concert tonight. _____

10. The school year begins on Wednesday August 27 and ends on Tuesday June 16. _____

11. We spotted a bald eagle a grizzly bear and many caribou during our vacation. _____

12. "The lettuce for the salad" said Mother "is in the fridge." _____

CHAPTER 7
Characters and Setting

• Complete the second column of the chart by matching each pair of characters to a likely setting. Then write an animal charcteristic that might figure into a trickster tale featuring each pair of characters.

crab and sea star	farmer and crow	cat and canary
roadrunner and coyote	salmon and bear	mongoose and cobra
polar bear and seal	giraffe and lion	

Setting	Character Pair	Animal Characteristic
1. a jungle in India	_____	_____ _____
2. an ocean tide pool	_____	_____ _____
3. an Arctic ice floe	_____	_____ _____
4. a house in the city	_____	_____ _____
5. a cornfield on a farm	_____	_____ _____
6. a Canadian river	_____	_____ _____

• On a separate sheet of paper, choose one of the character pairs that you didn't use in the chart and write a setting and an animal characteristic that might figure into a trickster tale.

CHAPTER 7
Exclamation Points and Question Marks

● **Add exclamation points, question marks, and periods where needed.**

1. Wow What a noisy pet store this is

2. Do you know how the badger got its name

3. What an amazing concert that was

4. What is the job of a milliner

5. That is such a good joke

6. Hurry The soup is boiling over

7. Yes I would love to attend the festival for free

8. Am I really the winner

9. Have the students returned their permission slips

10. That was the best day ever

11. Is James ready to go

12. Watch out

13. Oh my I dropped the glass

14. Can you lift that boulder

15. Stop The parrot might escape

CHAPTER 7

Semicolons

● **Write *correct* if the semicolon is used correctly or *incorrect* if it is not. Rewrite all incorrect sentences properly, deleting words if necessary.**

1. Vanessa cooked the spaghetti; and Michael made the sauce.   _____

_____

2. The lengthy movie ended; people rushed to leave the theater.   _____

_____

3. The gymnast aced the back handspring, the gold medal
was hers.   _____

_____

4. The sound of hammers filled the air; building had begun.   _____

_____

5. I love popcorn as a snack; but I really like it with cheese.   _____

_____

● **Rewrite each simple sentence as a compound sentence by adding an independent clause joined by a semicolon. The first one is done for you.**

6. Wendy is a talented painter.

Wendy is a talented painter; she has sold many of her works.

7. The traffic signals are not working.

_____

8. New Zealand is the home of many birds.

_____

9. The students followed all the directions.

_____

CHAPTER 7 Dialog

● **Write an appropriate dialog tag to complete each sentence.**

1. "These are my clothes, and I want you to leave them alone," my older sister _____ .

2. "Oh, Mom!" I _____ . "Why do I always have to go first?"

3. "Drop and give me twenty, soldier!" the sergeant _____ angrily.

4. "Do you know what this message means?" the detective _____ .

5. "Shhh," Mariah _____ . "I think I hear someone behind us."

● **Read the situation below. Write several lines of dialog that are engaging and help develop each character.**

Mouse and Rabbit eat the same foods and live in the same field. They spend most of their time together arguing. When Python moves into their territory, however, they realize that they must work together to stay alive. Through some clever trickery, they entice Python to leave.

_____

_____

_____

_____

_____

_____

_____

_____

CHAPTER 7

Colons

● **Add colons where needed. Write *salutation* or *list* to identify the colon rule illustrated in each sentence.**

1. Dear Mr. Clarke _____

2. Please purchase the following caramels, crackers, apples. _____

3. Arrange these names alphabetically Marci, Sam, Lee, and Harry. _____

4. To Whom It May Concern _____

5. Dear Ms. McKenna and Associates _____

6. Ryan entered these items into the computer names, ages, and addresses. _____

● **Rewrite each phrase by adding a list of examples, a colon, and end punctuation where necessary. The first one is done for you.**

7. For our camping trip bring the following items

   For our camping trip bring the following items: a sleeping bag, a canteen, and a flashlight.

8. We saw the following waterfowl on the lake

   _____

9. Our family owns three automobiles

   _____

10. To complete my art project, I will need the following

    _____

11. I regularly play three sports

    _____

12. The twins brought these items on their trip

    _____

CHAPTER 7

Quotation Marks

● **Complete the phrase to explain the use of the quotation marks in each sentence.**

1. "Look at the colors on that macaw!" exclaimed Sally.

   to _____

2. Ogden Nash wrote the humorous poem "The Hippopotamus."

   to _____

3. My father read "One Company Succeeds" in *U.S.A. Today*.

   to _____

4. "My new neighbors," explained Pam, "are from Michigan."

   to _____

● **Rewrite each sentence. Add quotation marks and underlining where needed.**

5. The teacher said, The field trip will be held next Friday.

   _____

6. Jack, he called, why don't you answer?

   _____

7. I read the poem A Distant View in the magazine Expressions of Memory.

   _____

8. The Wizard of Oz is my brother's favorite movie.

   _____

9. The Pit and the Pendulum is a classic short story.

   _____

10. I am looking for the latest issue of Sports Illustrated.

   _____

CHAPTER
7

Homographs

● **Match a homograph from the word box to each pair of definitions.**

| dove | swallow | lead | present | pupils | band |

1. _____	A. a strip of material used to tie or hold things B. a group of musicians
2. _____	A. a type of bird B. to pass into the stomach through the throat
3. _____	A. the openings in the eyes through which light passes B. young people who are being taught
4. _____	A. to show or direct along or through B. a heavy, dark, gray, fairly soft metal
5. _____	A. a type of bird B. plunged headfirst into the water
6. _____	A. to introduce one person to another B. a gift

● **Use a pair of homographs from above to complete each sentence.**
Write _A_ or _B_ to show which definition is being used.

1. The principal will first _____ our speaker; then Mr.
   Chang will give her the _____ .

2. We watched as the kingfisher _____ into the water while
   a _____ cooed from a branch overhead.

3. The _____ caught a fly and proceeded to _____ it.

4. The astonished _____ stared at the experiment; their
   _____ enlarged in the darkened room.

5. "Anthony, you _____ and we'll follow," Terry said as she
   drew out the route with a _____ pencil.

6. The members of the _____ were wearing a
   _____ around their left arms in protest.

CHAPTER 7

Apostrophes

- **Rewrite the words, using an apostrophe to show possession or to form a contraction.**

1. have not   _____   2. you are   _____

3. belonging to Paul   _____   4. belonging to the children   _____

5. will not   _____   6. could not   _____

7. I am   _____   8. possession of Carla   _____

- **Use a word you wrote above to complete each sentence. In the right-hand column write correctly any other item or items that need an apostrophe.**

9. The _____ school bus arrives at 8 oclock.   _____

10. The note from _____ mom is hard to read; her
    *g*s and *j*s look alike.   _____

11. We dont know what to do because you _____
    passed out the directions.   _____

12. _____ not the last in line, but Im going to be.   _____

13. The children wouldve loved to play with _____
    new pet.   _____

14. Mind your *p*s and *q*s or you _____ be getting
    any dessert!   _____

15. _____ putting away the dishes; Sarahs brother
    is helping me.   _____

16. My grandfather _____ attend the reunion of the
    class of 44.   _____

CHAPTER
7

Hyphens

● **Use hyphens to show where each word could be divided when breaking a word at the end of a line. Use a dictionary if you need help.**

1. imagine _____

2. instruments _____

3. unusual _____

4. embarrass _____

5. mosaic _____

6. needle _____

7. separate _____

8. sausage _____

● **Rewrite each sentence, adding hyphens where needed.**

9. That's a well known card trick.

_____

10. This April I will be twenty five years old.

_____

11. Our new neighbor seems good natured.

_____

12. Her mother in law is an attorney in Chicago.

_____

13. Blue forget me nots are blooming in my garden.

_____

14. Those guitar picks are seventy five cents each.

_____

15. The student is truly self motivated to succeed.

_____

16. Jake is tired of wearing his brother's hand me downs.

_____

CHAPTER 7

Rhyming Stanzas

● **Write as many rhyming words as you can for each word.**

1. allow _____

2. feel _____

3. here _____

4. star _____

5. rhyme _____

● **Choose two or more pairs of rhyming words from above. Then compose a short poem using the words you chose in a rhyming stanza. Use a rhyme scheme in your poem.**

_____

_____

_____

_____

_____

_____

● **Use the poem you wrote above to answer the questions.**

6. How many syllables are in the first line? _____

7. How many stanzas does your poem have? _____

8. What rhyme scheme did you use? _____

CHAPTER 7

Capital Letters

● Use the proofreader's mark (≡) to show the letters that should be capitalized in each sentence below. Then choose corresponding capitalization rules from the box and write them on the line to show why you added the capital letters.

Rules

pronoun *I*	section of the country
first word of sentence	first word of direct quotation
proper name of person	proper name of place
title of book	title before a name
proper adjective	title of poem

1. in the west the climate is arid, and water is scarce.

   _____

2. As i often say, "to have a friend, you need to be one."

   _____

3. The nelsons took a trip to monterey, california.

   _____

4. did paige read steinbeck's *of mice and men* and frost's "birches" last summer?

   _____

5. My grandfather served under general George Patton.

   _____

6. I heard that dennis hudson will attend the university of texas this fall.

   _____

7. A swedish student is visiting our cousins, the wiesners.

   _____

Name_____ Date_____

Self-Assessment

● Check *Always*, *Sometimes*, or *Never* to respond to each statement.

Writing	Always	Sometimes	Never
I can identify a trickster tale and its features.			
I understand how to develop the characters and the setting in a trickster tale.			
I include all key features when I write a trickster tale.			
I can create dialog to develop characters and plot.			
I can identify homographs and use them correctly.			
I can identify and write poetry with rhyming stanzas.			

Grammar	Always	Sometimes	Never
I can identify and use conjunctions.			
I can identify and use interjections.			
I can identify and use periods and abbreviations.			
I can identify and use commas.			
I can identify and use exclamation points and question marks.			
I can identify and use semicolons.			
I can identify and use colons.			
I can identify and use quotation marks.			
I can identify and use apostrophes.			
I can identify and use hyphens.			
I can identify when to use capital letters.			

● Describe how what you learned in this chapter will help you be a better writer.

_____

_____

_____

_____

CHAPTER 8 · Subjects and Predicates

● **Diagram the sentences.**

1. The students are reading.

2. Geese flew overhead.

3. The young child laughed.

4. The last patient waited quietly.

CHAPTER 8

Direct Objects
and Indirect Objects

● **Diagram the sentences.**

1. The author writes mystery stories.

2. I sent my grandmother a birthday card.

3. Thomas gave his neighbor some apples.

4. Several students finished their reports.

CHAPTER 8

What Makes a Good Research Report?

● **Read each statement. Circle *T* if the statement is true or *F* if it is false. Then rewrite each false statement to make it true.**

1. A research report is a form of fiction writing.   T   F

_____

2. A research report presents factual information in an organized manner.   T   F

_____

3. You do not need to research your facts if you know what you are talking about.   T   F

_____

4. When writing a research report, use a broad topic so information is easy to find.   T   F

_____

5. Sources are places you go to find information.   T   F

_____

6. Any Web site is considered a good source for information.   T   F

_____

7. A thesis statement is a sentence that briefly describes the main idea of a report.   T   F

_____

8. Unlike other types of writing, report writing does not require an introduction, a body, and a conclusion.   T   F

_____

_____

Subject Complements

● **Diagram the sentences.**

1. Golf is a difficult sport.

2. White roses are my favorite flower.

3. The roasted potatoes tasted too salty.

4. My stubborn brother remained unconvinced.

CHAPTER
8

Appositives

● **Diagram the sentences.**

1. His mother, a famous artist, sketches portraits.

2. Our family hiked the Rubicon Grade, a steep trail.

3. The winner was Mr. Tilly, our coach.

4. My aunt prepared tamales, a favorite dish.

Gathering and Organizing Information

CHAPTER 8

● **Cross out any choice that does not correctly complete each statement.**

1. When taking notes you should
   a. write down the important things you find out about your topic.
   b. write all information, except direct quotations, in your own words.
   c. use quotation marks when recording a quote you would like to use.
   d. write only sensory words that create a visual image in your mind.
   e. write a research question that answers a given fact or idea.

2. When organizing your notes you might
   a. use assorted scraps of paper and store them in boxes.
   b. write each piece of information on an index card.
   c. review your notes to see if you want or need to revise your thesis.
   d. group ideas and facts together by question, topic, or subtopic.
   e. trade cards with a partner until you have the facts you need.

3. When using your notes you should
   a. not actually look at them when you write your report.
   b. place ideas that no longer fit your thesis in a separate pile.
   c. arrange your note cards to create an outline.
   d. never change your thesis topic.
   e. review the organized information to be sure it still fits your thesis.

● **For each statement, write a possible topic that it might be used for.**

4. Butterflies have a feeding tube called a proboscis. They have no mandibles.

   _____

5. The Egyptians built wooden sailing ships after 2700 BC that were capable of sea voyages.

   _____

CHAPTER 8

Intensive and Reflexive Pronouns

● **Diagram the sentences.**

1. The puppy shook itself vigorously.

2. I myself played a solo performance.

3. The twins completed the project themselves.

4. Mrs. Fielding bought herself a new dress.

CHAPTER 8

Prepositional Phrases as Modifiers

● **Diagram the sentences.**

1. The man in the blue sweater is my uncle.

2. The swim team practiced at the lake.

3. Many children in my class ride on the bus.

4. The chocolate candies in the jar taste terrible.

CHAPTER 8 Citing Sources

- **Write *encyclopedia, book,* or *Web site* to identify the source of each citation.**

1. "King Richard III." <u>The World Book Encyclopedia</u>. 2000 edition.

_____

2. Becket, Carrie. <u>1001 Useful Knots</u>. Annapolis, MD: First Light Publishers, 1995.

_____

3. Pak, Terry. "Kitchen Chemistry." 3 Sep. 2004 <www.chemistrymatters.org/kitchen_htm>.

_____

4. "Lake Tahoe." <u>New Book of Knowledge</u>. 2002 edition.

_____

5. Bennett, Clark. <u>Indians of the United States</u>. Portland, OR: Timber Press, 1999.

_____

6. "Artifacts of the House Chamber." 16 Aug. 2002 <www.clerk.house.gov/Artifacts.html>.

_____

7. Sanchez, Rene. "Prairie Coneflower." <u>Encyclopedia of Perennial Plants</u>. 2nd edition. 2004.

_____

- **Write an entry for a Works Cited page based on the information from the copyright page.**

PREDATORY BIRDS OF THE SOUTHWEST DESERT

Sunrise Books, Inc.
1000 Maddox Ave, Santa Fe, NM 00000

Copyright © 1999 by William Santos
All rights reserved
Printed in the United States of America
First edition, 1999

8. _____

_____

CHAPTER
8

Compound Sentence Parts

● **Diagram the sentences.**

1. Theresa and her mother shopped at the mall.

2. A tennis ball fell and rolled between the cars.

3. Maurice and I will leave at noon.

4. My sister and I washed the dishes and cleaned the sink.

CHAPTER 8

Compound Sentences

● **Diagram the sentences.**

1. Susan wanted tomato soup, but her sister preferred spicy chili.

2. The children can paint with watercolors, or they can play outside.

3. The desert is basically dry, yet many flowers grow there.

4. Grandfather opened the door, and we ran up the steps.

CHAPTER 8

Roots

● **Use your understanding of roots to match each word with its definition.**

1. geotropism _____

2. extract _____

3. audition _____

4. anachronism _____

5. dynamometer _____

6. contradict _____

7. retractile _____

8. missionary _____

a. capable of being pulled back again

b. the growth of a living thing in response to Earth's gravity

c. one who is sent to do charitable or religious work

d. to pull out forcibly

e. an instrument used to measure mechanical power

f. the act of hearing a trial performance

g. something that is out of its proper order or time

h. to speak in an opposite manner

● **Choose four words from above. Correctly use each of them in a sentence. Use a dictionary if you need help.**

9. _____

_____

10. _____

_____

11. _____

_____

12. _____

_____

CHAPTER 8 Interjections

● **Diagram the sentences.**

1. Wow! I love your new bike.

2. Shush! The baby is finally sleeping.

3. Hooray! We won first prize.

4. Ouch! I hit my head on the shelf.

CHAPTER

8

Adverb Clauses

● **Diagram the sentences.**

1. After you finish college, you will find a good job.

2. Sam takes the bus because he does not have a car.

3. Mother watched her favorite movie while she folded the clean laundry.

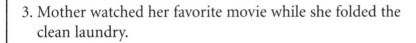

4. Although I had never played before, I got the highest score.

Using the Library and the Internet

● Write *encyclopedia, atlas,* or *almanac* to identify the best source for each piece of information.

1. Nations that border Austria _____

2. Top 10 states by population in 2001 _____

3. Highest mountain peak in the state of Montana _____

4. Main agricultural exports of Argentina _____

5. Early methods of telling time _____

6. 2004 listing of U.S. best-selling magazines _____

● Write *library, Internet,* or *both* to identify which source each statement describes.

7. Includes an area of reference books that generally cannot be checked out _____

8. May have a computerized or card catalog _____

9. Type in a keyword to locate information on a specific topic _____

10. New information can be posted immediately _____

11. Uses a search engine to locate subjects or topics _____

12. If a search does not turn up any results, your topic might be too specialized _____

13. Uses call numbers to organize information by subject _____

14. The extension of the address may be an indicator of the reliability of the information _____

CHAPTER 8 Diagramming Review

● **Diagram the sentences.**

1. Taffy, a stray cat, ran quickly behind the cardboard box.

2. My sister bought a new jacket, and she wore it to the party.

3. Ryan and Jackie watched the basketball game while their mom baked oatmeal cookies.

4. Yikes! I myself left the money on the table.

CHAPTER

8 Self-Assessment

● **Check *Always*, *Sometimes*, or *Never* to respond to each statement.**

Writing	Always	Sometimes	Never
I can identify the features of a research report.			
I understand how to take, organize, and use notes.			
I can identify and cite sources.			
I can use my knowledge of roots to understand the meaning of words.			
I understand how to use the library and the Internet when I write a research report.			
I include all the key features when I write a research report.			

Grammar	Always	Sometimes	Never
I can diagram subjects and predicates in sentences.			
I can diagram sentences with direct and indirect objects.			
I can diagram sentences with subject complements.			
I can diagram sentences with appositives.			
I can diagram sentences with intensive and reflexive pronouns.			
I can diagram sentences with prepositional phrases.			
I can diagram compound elements in sentences.			
I can diagram compound sentences.			
I can diagram sentences with interjections.			
I can diagram sentences with adverb clauses.			

● **Explain how learning to diagram the parts of sentences in this chapter will help you be a better writer.**

_____

_____

_____

_____

_____

Word/Idea Web

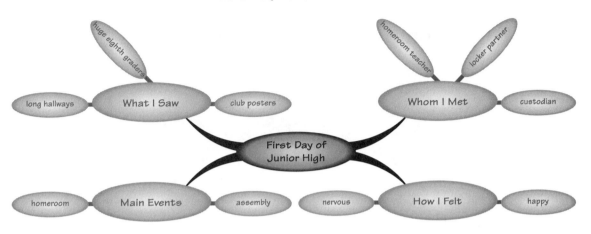

Narrative Map

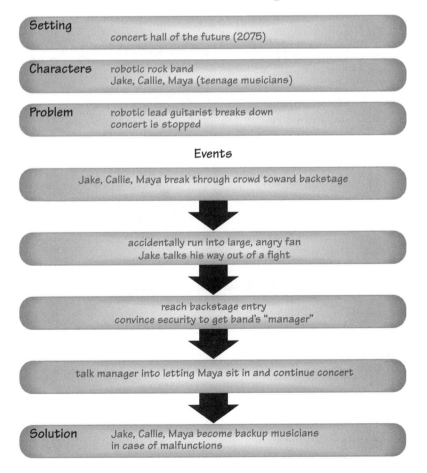

Setting concert hall of the future (2075)

Characters robotic rock band
Jake, Callie, Maya (teenage musicians)

Problem robotic lead guitarist breaks down
concert is stopped

Events

Jake, Callie, Maya break through crowd toward backstage

accidentally run into large, angry fan
Jake talks his way out of a fight

reach backstage entry
convince security to get band's "manager"

talk manager into letting Maya sit in and continue concert

Solution Jake, Callie, Maya become backup musicians
in case of malfunctions

Compare and Contrast Chart

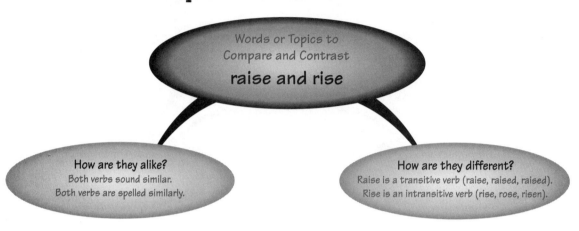

Words or Topics to Compare and Contrast
raise and rise

How are they alike?
Both verbs sound similar.
Both verbs are spelled similarly.

How are they different?
Raise is a transitive verb (raise, raised, raised).
Rise is an intransitive verb (rise, rose, risen).

Word Analysis Chart

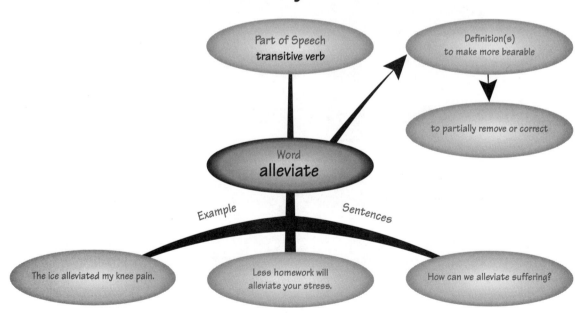

Part of Speech
transitive verb

Definition(s)
to make more bearable

to partially remove or correct

Word
alleviate

Example

Sentences

The ice alleviated my knee pain.

Less homework will alleviate your stress.

How can we alleviate suffering?

Steps in a Process Chart

Title: Egg Basket Cupcakes

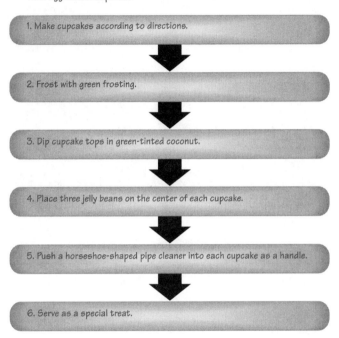

1. Make cupcakes according to directions.

2. Frost with green frosting.

3. Dip cupcake tops in green-tinted coconut.

4. Place three jelly beans on the center of each cupcake.

5. Push a horseshoe-shaped pipe cleaner into each cupcake as a handle.

6. Serve as a special treat.

Paragraph Plan

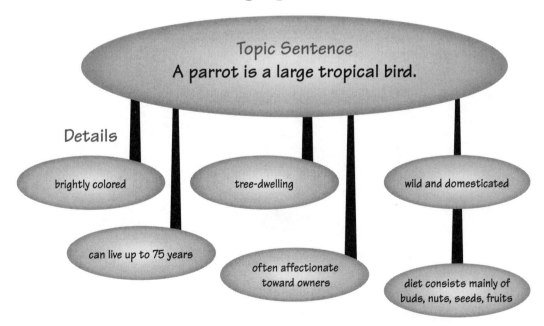

Topic Sentence
A parrot is a large tropical bird.

Details

brightly colored

tree-dwelling

wild and domesticated

can live up to 75 years

often affectionate toward owners

diet consists mainly of buds, nuts, seeds, fruits

Problem and Solution Chart

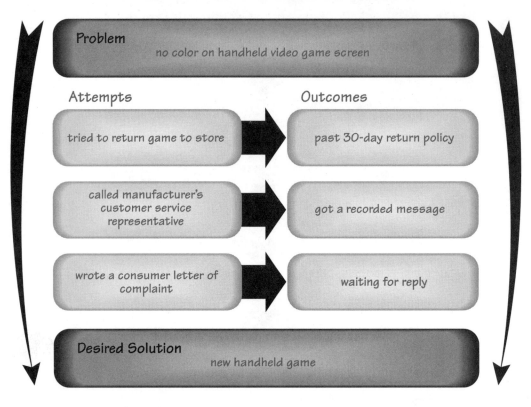

Problem
no color on handheld video game screen

Attempts

Outcomes

tried to return game to store → past 30-day return policy

called manufacturer's customer service representative → got a recorded message

wrote a consumer letter of complaint → waiting for reply

Desired Solution
new handheld game

Cause and Effect Chart

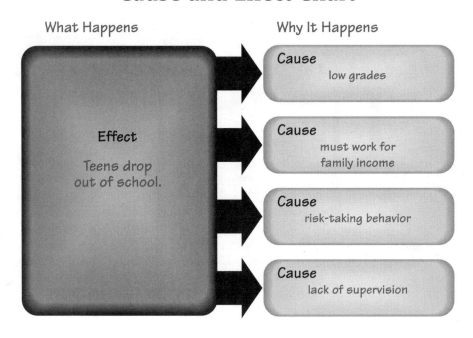

What Happens

Why It Happens

Effect

Teens drop out of school.

Cause
low grades

Cause
must work for family income

Cause
risk-taking behavior

Cause
lack of supervision